Praise for *No Reservations*

"This is a must-read for anyone in the service industry, where the great differentiator in a world filled with generic products is PEOPLE who are truly willing to SERVE. *No Reservations* provides the blueprint for those looking to build customer loyalty, one relationship at a time."
—JON GORDON, author of *The Energy Bus* and *Soup*

"If you want to be inspired to live better, lead better, and leave a legacy that matters, read this book."
—JIMMY PAGE, Vice President, Fellowship of Christian Athletes, and best-selling author of *One Word That Will Change Your Life* and *WisdomWalks*

"*No Reservations* does for the Service Industry what Eliyahu Goldratt's, *The Goal*, did for manufacturing. Practical wisdom that can help any organization refocus on what it takes to deliver truly exceptional service experiences."
—GREG VAN SCOY, Senior Vice President, Burke, Inc., Research Specialists in Employee Engagement & Customer Loyalty

"*No Reservations* quickly gets to the heart of the importance and value of creating an exceptional customer experience. It is packed full of practical examples of how each employee can contribute to their own personal success as well as the success of their organization. *No Reservations* reinforces the fact that with the right leadership and attitude, your company culture can change for the better."
—BARRY HIMMEL, Senior Vice President, Signature Worldwide—Customer Experience Training Specialists

"The best investment a company can make is in customer service and satisfaction. The payoff not only is great for our customers, but for our companies and employees, as well. *No Reservations* is a shining example of this principle."
—DORA BOURGAULT, Owner/Operator,
Park Avenue Travel Services

"*No Reservations* is full of very practical and sound advice. It's sure to be a winner."
—GEORGE CECIL, CEO,
Biltmore Farms, Inc.

"I recommend *No Reservations* because Todd writes about the way he lives and what he believes in. His positiveness and friendliness manifest themselves in this story of customer service and employee satisfaction. Everyone can benefit from reading this book." —ROY BALDWIN, President,
Got Your Back Network

"Todd lives out the message in *No Reservations*. I have seen his 'People Before Profits' philosophy displayed in his selfless giving to others, his impeccable character, and his compassionate care for others. I count him as a true mentor and friend." —GREG BLAKE, CEO, Pepworks, Inc.

No Reservations

A STORY ABOUT BUILDING CUSTOMER LOYALTY
ONE RELATIONSHIP AT A TIME

Todd Gothberg

Published by
R. Brent and Company
Asheville NC • rbrent.com

Published in Asheville, North Carolina
by R. Brent and Company
50 Deerwood Drive
Asheville NC 28805
rbrent.com

Editor and publisher: *Robbin Brent Whittington*
Editorial consultant: *Jane Ware*
Cover design: *jb graphics, Asheville, North Carolina*
Cover photo*: *Bonnie Krebs*
Author photo on back cover and p. 127: *Thompson Photography, Gettysburg, Pennsylvania*
Compositor: *Rick Soldin, Blountville, Tennessee*
Illustrations: *jb graphics, Asheville, North Carolina*
The inn featured on the cover and in the book is The Balsam Mountain Inn, tucked in the Blue Ridge Mountains
 balsammountaininn.net • 800-224-9498

Library of Congress Cataloging-in-Publication Data

Gothberg, Todd, 1964–
  No reservations: a story about building customer loyalty one
relationship at a time / Todd Gothberg. —First edition.
      p.   cm.
   ISBN 978-0-9788160-9-4 (paperback)
   ISBN 978-0-9910398-0-7 (e-book)
   1. Employee Engagement   2. Organizational Change   3. Inspiration
   I. Title
                                                  2013953448

Printed in the United States of America.

17 16 15 14   6 5 4 3
Second printing

Todd Gothberg may be contacted at toddgothberg@gmail.com for ordering information. This book is also available for order online at toddgothberg.com, or amazon.com. This book has been published as an e-book, and is available at amazon.com.

For my daughters, who have always
inspired me to be my very best self.
I thank God daily for the gift of your lives.
—T.M.G.

Contents

Acknowledgements

First and foremost, I'm thankful to God for His gifts of writing, speaking, and inspiring. Life is no solo act, and this book is the result of experiences and relationships that He has intentionally guided.

I'm thankful for my friend, Jon Gordon, who has modeled the way and inspired my writing with his life example and amazing books. *The Energy Bus* has had an incredible ripple effect upon the lives of so many, and the impact that this book has had on my life simply cannot be measured.

So thankful for the support and encouragement of Brooke Trabert, Jon's Chief Relationship Officer. Her belief that my book would come to fruition never wavered, even when I had my own doubts.

To friends Drew Darnell, Tony den Hoed, and Cyndy Chepak-Cooper. Thanks for holding me accountable to the Vision, and for the consistent check-ins and challenges that helped ensure this story moved from my heart to reality.

Many thanks to my friend and publisher, Robbin Whittington, for her counsel, support, and encouragement.

Deep appreciation to Charles Ewers and Norma Walrath, my Creative Writing and Journalism teachers at Ledyard High School in Ledyard, Connecticut, for believing in me and instructing in such a way that writing became a passion.

Thankful for my best friend, Lorne Day, whose leadership and reading example sparked this journey so many years ago.

To my mentor, hero, and life coach, Bill Sauber, for his unrelentingly consistent friendship, love, and support. His Legacy continues to impact my life.

To Catherine Purdy and Jill Goldie, so thankful for their professional examples at Volvo Construction Equipment, examples that formed characters in this book and inspired the foundation for this story.

Special thanks to dear friends Jenny Guy and Dr. Lisa Greene for their respective faith walks and life examples.

To my mom for her unconditional love, spirit, and perseverance.

Thankful for my dad for instilling my faith, social conscience, and passion for life.

Emily, Alissa, Rylee, and Caroline Gothberg. Thanks for being the reason I do what I do.

Finally, I am beyond blessed and thankful for Camp Calumet Lutheran and my friends from that magical place in New Hampshire, all who have shaped and shared my life for nearly fifty years. We all are because Calumet = Love.

1. Reservations

As exciting and rewarding as this new opportunity might shape up to be, Rob harbored some serious reservations about the assignment. With the small commuter plane making its final descent into the airport, his thoughts raced back to a conversation he had had with his boss just two weeks before. "We need you in North Carolina, Rob. Big issues are brewing in the mountains," said Emily Ferguson, Rob's boss. She had flown to Chicago to meet with him at The Harper, the hotel he helped manage just off Lake Shore Drive.

As part of a strong leadership team, he had it made—a prime job at a top-shelf hotel in an idyllic location. Occupancy rates and customer satisfaction metrics consistently exceeded expectations, and employee satisfaction was among the highest of any Harper property in the nation. Five years ago he had moved from the East Coast to accept an assignment in the Windy City, becoming part of a finely tuned team that had flourished under Emily's strong leadership. Emily's reward for her time in Chicago was a promotion to

Vice President of U.S. Hotel Operations. It had been almost effortless to ride Emily's legacy of excellence at The Harper. She had hired an outstanding executive team that had, in turn, assembled an amazing array of talent to run the hotel.

When Rob stepped in, he quickly realized that his role was primarily to keep things headed in the right direction, maintain the status quo, and to learn as much as possible from the members of the executive team. Emily believed that Rob had the energy, the passion, and the determination to succeed on his own; the only thing he lacked was the practical experience, which she knew he couldn't get until someone who believed in him gave him a shot. For five years in Chicago, Rob had been a sponge, taking in everything while fine-tuning his leadership skills. Skills he'd been fortunate to cultivate during some very good economic times when business was booming, the economy was rolling along, and the mood on the street was about as good as it gets. But now, as everyone knew, those times were a thing of the past.

The excitement he felt on the threshold of this new assignment came from prior success and his readiness to prove himself as a leader. Yet, the level of his excitement was matched by his reservations that The Harper in North Carolina might be beyond salvage. He simply didn't know if what he'd learned to date was enough to help course-correct a property in a potentially lethal nose-dive. Those flush times in Chicago now seemed light years behind him as he was about to land in an unfamiliar town and an unfamiliar situation, his stellar team and his wife and children hundreds of miles away.

Rob was about to learn that leadership lessons during good, stable times rarely are enough to prepare one to lead in and through a storm.

2. Reality Sets In

As Rob waited for his luggage at baggage claim, he recalled what Emily had told him about the North Carolina property—and most of it wasn't good. She started out with the positives: beautiful location, a popular retirement and vacation destination, friendly people, and a host of activities for the outdoor enthusiast. She knew that, while his time in the Midwest had been enjoyable, Rob missed the mountains. Growing up in New England, he had spent his summers in New Hampshire and Maine and developed a love of the outdoors. The same mountains he hiked in the summer became fertile grounds for skiing as fall turned to winter. Winter weather in the Midwest brought snow, ice, cold, and nasty winds—but no mountains. From what he had heard, this new town was chock-full of incredible biking and running trails. Yet, he found himself wondering if he would have any time to enjoy the beauty of his new surroundings in light of the challenges Emily was telling him he would be facing.

According to Emily, the list of downsides was about as ugly as it gets: rock-bottom employee morale, the worst customer satisfaction ratings for any Harper property in the U.S., high staff turnover, and some of the lowest occupancy rates in the region. Add to all this the current economic climate, and Rob knew he was quite literally walking into a nightmare. Check that. He was *inheriting* a nightmare, and he had six months to turn things around. Emily had shared, in confidence, that The Harper Properties Board had decided—somewhat reluctantly—to give her one last shot at making this location viable. If the property did not start turning a profit in six months, the board had reached consensus that they would begin looking for a buyer. And even if they did see a return to profitability, they still reserved the right to sell. Truthfully, Emily did not hold out much hope, which is why she hadn't recruited a more seasoned leader to turn things around. A part of her believed that there probably wasn't much anyone could do at this point, other than to begin, as gracefully as possible, shutting things down and preparing for the sale.

But there was another part of her that believed this could be the perfect situation for Rob. Nobody expected a miracle, and it would be almost impossible to tarnish his reputation. None of the reasons for failure would stick to him. And if, by some wild chance, he was successful in doing the impossible, Rob would become a candidate to follow in her footsteps when she was promoted to her next assignment. She knew that one of the greatest legacies a leader can leave behind is the legacy of what those whom they lead and mentor go on to become and to achieve.

During the discussion about this "opportunity," Rob had asked how things had gotten so bad. Was it a gradual decline, or did things spiral downward quickly? Was one person to blame, or was there enough blame to go around multiple times? Was any staff worth keeping, or should he just clean house? Were there several root causes, or was it one specific issue driving the measurable results downward? Emily was intentional, but vague, in her responses. "You'll need to figure these things out on your own," she had said. "I don't want to influence or prejudice your perspective going in. I will tell you that we have replaced the site manager and currently, there is no one overseeing the overall operations. I've asked my Southeast regional manager, Joe Sabol, to visit the property at least once a week until you arrive. He's also been instructed to meet you there on your first day to show you around and introduce you to the staff. He's also available to you throughout the six months on an as-needed basis."

Finally, Rob asked the inevitable question, "Is this a one-way ticket if I can't turn things around?" Emily reassured him that there would always be a place for him, but at the same time she was clear that he needed to *think* and *act* as if the umbilical cord had been cut. He needed to take a "burn the ships" philosophy—a reference to Spaniard explorer Cortez and his 1519 invasion of Mexico, when he commanded his men to burn the ships to ensure there were no other options other than to be successful executing the planned invasion. Rob thought the example was a little extreme, but he understood clearly the point she was making.

He thanked Emily for her honesty, and for her trust and belief in him. He asked for a few days to think through the offer—he needed to consult with his family and other trusted advisors and friends—before giving her his answer. But after several intense but quick phone calls and a conversation with his family, he called Emily the next day. Rob was all in.

3. Second Thoughts

After retrieving his bags, Rob picked up a rental car and a map that would get him to his new apartment. As he easily navigated the light traffic, he couldn't help but notice the stark contrast between the stability and permanence of his life in the Midwest and his new life in the mountains. One consolation in the midst of these drastic changes was that he had been provided an apartment spacious enough to accommodate his family whenever they could come down for a visit. Fortunately, the short, ten-minute drive from the airport didn't give him enough time to seriously think about getting on the next plane out of town to Chicago. But the thought did cross his mind, as did others. What was he thinking? Was he crazy? Life had been good in Chicago. Was he up to the task at hand? Why had they picked him? And, how was he going to manage without his family by his side?

He sorely missed his wife and daughters. The plan was for them to wrap up the school year in Chicago and then join him just in time for the summer—IF things looked like they were headed in the right direction. If things still looked bleak, they'd sit tight through the summer and, in all likelihood, he'd get a new assignment just before school started in the fall. Just as the last of these thoughts faded into his subconscious, he pulled up in front of his temporary residence, grabbed his bags, unlocked the door, and stepped into the large, fully furnished apartment. He had arrived.

After unloading and unpacking his bags, Rob decided to lace up his running shoes and get acquainted with his new surroundings, and acclimated to the much warmer North Carolina weather. No matter the time of year, he loved running for a number of reasons. Primarily, it energized him. Counterintuitive to what many people believed, Rob found that exercising actually gave him more energy, and even on those days when he didn't feel like going out, he did anyway, and afterwards always felt better. Running kept him healthy, kept the weight off, and allowed him to think more clearly about life's problems.

There were many times he'd head out on a run with no idea how he was going to solve a particular problem—personal or professional—and yet somehow, over the course of the run, the ideas and solutions would flow. It was almost a race back to his office or home to capture the thoughts before they escaped. This day's run would prove tougher than most for two reasons: the challenge ahead of him was weighing heavy on his mind and distracting his effort, and the altitude (just over 2,400 feet above sea level) would take some getting used to. Oh, and the hills. His lungs burned as his legs shuffled through his new surroundings. Resisting the urge, he chose neither to bag nor shorten the run. He pushed through until things felt easier, when the "runners high" kicked in.

As he settled into an easier rhythm and pace, he began to think through what was ahead. Where would he start? What would he say to the team on Monday? Would there be any-body aside from Joe to tap into, to gain insights that would help him prioritize tasks and action plans? Did any of this really matter? Eight miles later, Rob decided that was enough for today, worrying and running. Monday would come soon enough. And tomorrow was a new day.

4. Going on Faith

With Sunday morning came the search for a church to visit. Rob knew deep down that he wasn't going to be able to carry this load on his own. He needed spiritual guidance and he recognized that his faith had carried him through so many of life's previous challenges. If there was one thing he had learned along the way, it was the sustaining nature—during good times and the difficult times—of his relationship with, and his faith in, God. But this challenge, it seemed, was different. It felt bigger, scarier, and more overwhelming than any he'd taken on before. It was time to lean even harder on his faith. A good friend once told him that both fear and faith have something in common: they both believe in a future that hasn't yet happened.[1] The only difference is what that future looks like. Choosing to move forward on faith, not fear, would be an absolute necessity.

Rob found a church service to attend, and it seemed to more fully ground him. He suddenly felt more confident and capable and better equipped to address what was ahead on the professional front. Several members greeted him and made him feel at home, but still, it wasn't the same as attending his home church. He thought about his wife and daughters back home, knowing they'd be getting up soon and heading to church. Despite the fact that he missed them tremendously, he took comfort knowing they'd be surrounded by people who loved them.

Later that afternoon, Rob took some time to check out the town. It was just as beautiful as described. There was an energy, a really cool "vibe" to the small city in the mountains and he came to the conclusion that even if he were to fail at turning things around, he'd at least have six months

> *Choosing to move forward on faith, not fear, would be an absolute necessity.*

in an incredibly beautiful setting, enjoying any free time he could carve out for himself along the way. After a self-guided tour of his new surrounding, Rob called Joe to finalize a meeting place and time for Monday morning. Joe suggested that they meet for breakfast at seven so Rob could meet his first day with both an open mind and a semi-fortified spirit.

5. Monday

*U*sually Rob awoke before his alarm, but not today. His body clock still operating on central time, he struggled out of bed and laced up the running shoes he'd left bedside the night before. He took a few minutes to make the transition from the warmth and solitude of his bed, but it was still dark and he was tired as he shuffled down the steps and into the street to begin his run. He thought to himself that this was going to be one of those runs you get through, but you don't enjoy.

After his run and shower, Rob met up with Joe as planned for breakfast downtown. He didn't have much of an appetite as he was fighting nerves and last night's dinner, which wasn't agreeing with him. After a warm greeting and a fresh cup of coffee delivered by a smiling server, Joe asked where he would like to begin. Rob had learned a long time ago that there was a reason God gave him two ears and one mouth; you can learn so much more from listening than you can by talking. He asked Joe to tell him anything and everything that might be of value, and then he spent the better part of the hour letting Joe talk while he took copious notes.

He learned that things were much worse than Emily had described. Employees were leaving daily—and not just the poor performers. The hotel's reputation within the community and across the country on internet travel sites was going downhill fast. The Visitor's Bureau had de-listed the hotel from their website, no longer recommending the property for out-of-town travelers. Just last week, several conference meeting planners had pulled out of contracts with the hotel for upcoming events that had been planned more than a year in advance. It was alarming that people were willing to pay the cancellation fee and go through the last-minute gyrations of finding an alternative site to host a conference, rather than holding their meetings at The Harper. It couldn't get much uglier, but Joe clearly wasn't going to sugar-coat anything. He figured that Rob would come to know the truth and the ugly reality anyway, and he was already here, in town, committed to the assignment. Full disclosure was necessary. After he finished his bleak summary and answered all of Rob's initial questions, Joe insisted on picking up the check. He wanted to offer one small moment of pleasure and ease for Rob in light of what loomed on the horizon.

Rob followed Joe to The Harper Hotel. From the outside, it looked very similar to the Chicago property. It was beautifully designed, and he could tell that its exterior had received a fresh coat of paint within the year, the landscaping was impeccably neat and inviting, and the location was in a prime spot. The biggest difference, from the outside, was the lack of cars. Otherwise, things looked pretty normal. As is often the case, Rob had learned—whether it was a business, a church, or even families—everything could look wonderful on the outside while the things on the inside were falling apart. Initial appearances were often deceiving.

As Rob parked his car, he noticed the first thing that truly disturbed him. The parking spot closest to the front entrance, just to the side of the handicap parking spaces, had a sign posted in the ground at the head of the spot.

RESERVED
FOR
HOTEL MANAGER

"Wow!" Rob thought out loud, "are you kidding me?" He called over to Joe, who was just collecting his briefcase from his car, "What's up with this premium parking spot for the hotel manager? Whose grand idea was this?"

"I'm guessing it had something to do with the person who's no longer here!" Joe said, making a slight grimace.

Rob shared the reason for his reaction. Only a few months earlier, as he was passing a church during the running leg of a Triathlon, Rob noticed a sign for the parking spot closest to the church (just as close on the opposite side as the handicap spot!) that read:

RESERVED
FOR PASTOR

"So much for servant leadership," Rob said. "What kind of a message does it send to the church that the pastor would take the closest parking space? That ought to be reserved for visitors!" Rob was fairly sure he'd never attend a church that saved its best parking spot for the pastor. And he was convinced that any business that saved its prime parking spaces for top brass had things completely upside down. It really should be about the leader of any organization serving his or her people, not the other way around. Little things like that often send big messages.

"Joe, do me a favor, could we have the guy in charge of facilities and property management remove that sign today?"

Joe nodded in the affirmative and assured Rob that it would happen, sooner rather than later. He understood the issue and Rob's rationale, and no doubt agreed with the perspective, wondering silently to himself how it could have happened in the first place.

Rob followed Joe into the lobby of the property and quickly sensed that the inside didn't match the beauty of the outside. There were no smiles, no warm greeting, no energy, and for certain, the place lacked passion. In a word, it was lifeless. He had been in morgues that had more life. *It's no wonder employees no longer want to work here and guests don't want to spend the night with us*, Rob thought to himself. *This place is bringing me down, and I've only been here a few minutes!*

Rob searched for a friendly face, a reason to hope, to no avail. As they moved through the lobby and into the manager's office, Rob greeted those folks he encountered. He noticed name tags, and called the employees by name. He could tell that none of them were comfortable with management recognizing them as anything more than staff. Deep down, he inherently knew that needed to change. Quickly.

The manager's office was well appointed, with a beautiful black leather chair, mahogany desk and credenza, and what appeared to be some pretty expensive artwork. It was clear that someone spent most of his time in the office and not out in the hotel. Rob dropped his backpack, pulled out a notebook, and got ready for the tour. Despite his experience, he clearly had not been prepared for this.

6. Where To Start?

*R*ob's first stop was the front desk. It appeared to be unattended, or so he assumed. Sitting at a desk behind the counter was a young lady, busy texting someone, and chances were pretty strong that it *wasn't* a guest. He could see a *People* magazine sitting out, and the phone was ringing with no hope of being answered. A second front-desk attendant in the back room quickly came out front when he realized what was going on. Joe took the opportunity to introduce Rob to Janice and Ben, but neither seemed really enthusiastic or impressed with the new kid in town. At least they weren't until Joe explained who Rob was. It was amazing how quickly the attitudes changed. Their reaction and responses said it all, as far as Rob was concerned. *And these are my "Directors of First Impressions"?* Rob thought. Joe let Janice know that she needed to put her phone away and he asked Ben to deposit the *People* magazine in the trash can. It was time for the tour to move on.

On the way to the hotel's restaurant, Joe mentioned to Rob that just yesterday the hotel chef had tendered his resignation. The chef said that he simply no longer wanted to be associated with a hotel like The Harper. He had bigger aspirations and wanted to be part of something "World Class." He said that he had signed on a few years ago because he believed in the values and ideals of The Harper properties, and he had high hopes. But somewhere along the way, they had been dashed. Rob knew that when word hit the streets that Chef Carl had left, the restaurant side of the business would evaporate, just like the residency side of the business.

As Rob and Joe crossed the lobby and headed for the gift shop, Rob noticed that the basic things—a clean, shiny floor, polished counters, fresh plants, and dust-free tables—had been neglected. He excused himself and ducked into the lobby restroom. The joke back in Chicago about The Harper's public bathrooms was that while they were clean enough to eat in, there were far better places on the property to dine. But Rob quickly discovered that this property's bathroom was an embarrassment. The waste baskets were overflowing, one of the toilets was backed up, and the mirrors were streaked. It was obvious that nobody had tended to them recently, and even more obvious that nobody cared. Rob expressed his disappointment to Joe, who just shrugged and said something to the effect of, "I told you so," but his word choice was less sanitized.

The gift shop seemed the one bright spot on the tour thus far. When they arrived, they were greeted by a lady who went by the name, "Cat," which was short for Catherine. Cat had a smile that lit up the room. She was already standing as Rob and Joe approached, and greeted them both by name—she had done some prior due diligence and knew that Rob was coming. Every part of who she was seemed genuine. Her work area was spotless, and the gift shop was organized and appealing to the eye. Cat was immediately engaging and personable. After introductions and some polite and enjoyable small talk, Rob asked her how things were really going. She thought for a moment and then replied, "Great! While I recognize that these are tough times and we've got some critically important things to address, I want you to know that I'm here to do my part and I want to be part of the solution. I'm committed to this place and I have faith in a better future."

Rob *loved* her attitude, and her energy. He later learned that she had retired from a local manufacturing firm and wasn't ready to walk away from work for good. She loved being around people and she understood that every customer interaction provided her with yet another opportunity to leave a legacy. Rob thanked Cat for her passion and for being part of the team, assuring her that he'd be back soon to take her up on her offer to help with the turnaround effort.

Joe decided it was time to take Rob to "The Dungeon," as it was not-so-affectionately known; it was the place the housekeeping staff gathered first thing in the morning to start their day. The room was poorly lighted, in need of a new coat of paint, and the furniture was a hodge-podge collection of broken pieces pulled together from the property over the years. It was obvious to Rob that this would be a good place to start his "make-over." By this time, all of the housekeeping staff were out on the floors. He noticed the smell and a trail of smoke coming from a back office, and he followed it to the housekeeping manager's office.

With her feet planted atop her desk, a cigarette in her hand, and her eyes focused on the small TV behind her desk, Carla looked about as comfortable as she could get. As he entered the room, Joe made one of those voice-clearing noises that generally act as a warning shot across the bow to announce someone's arrival. Carla did not move. This was her domain, and nobody was going to interrupt her break time.

"Carla, I'd like to introduce you to our new General Manager."

Carla slowly rotated the swivel chair around, put her cigarette down in the ash tray, and acknowledged the visitors. "Well, thank you both for stopping by my area, but as you can see I'm pretty busy this morning and need to begin checking the work of my ladies. So if you'll excuse me ..." And with that, Carla was gone.

"Beautiful, eh?" commented Joe. "She's been here for as long as anyone can remember. At one time she ran a tight ship, and knows everything there is to know about a clean room. I think in her day, she even held some record for the fastest room cleaning. She was good. Somewhere along the way, she was promoted from housekeeper to manager—not sure by who, but I'm pretty sure since she was the best housekeeper, someone figured she'd make a great manager of housekeeping. Obviously, she's a case in point that this philosophy isn't always a sound one.

The next tour stop was a walk through the floors, hallways, and guest rooms. Each housekeeper looked busy enough, their individual carts parked right outside the room they were cleaning. Rob noticed one consistent thing about each of the ladies he encountered: none wore a smile. With heads down, shoulders slumped, and robot-like movements, each housekeeper went about her work in a passionless manner. There was no idle chit-chat, no banter between them, just people putting in time. Rob had noticed earlier in the tour, in the housekeeping break room, a series of check marks on a wall almost in countdown format. It was clear to him now, putting two and two together, that at least one of the employees was counting the days until retirement. He watched as the ladies did just what they had to, and nothing more. Each cart had a list of tasks to be completed for each room, nothing more, nothing less. The goal was to finish quickly, but not at the expense of a clean room.

One of the problems, Joe explained, was that turnover in housekeeping was more than eighty percent annually. The only people who had more than a year's worth of experience were folks who had nowhere else to go—they were locked in for one reason or another. Some relied on public transportation to get to/from work. In this down economy, most others recognized that nobody else was hiring. Rob believed, based upon what he had heard through the grapevine and through select exit interviews, that nobody could handle working for Carla. She was a tyrant known for nasty mood-swings, someone who sucked the life out of her workers and, ultimately, the organization. With turnover peaking under her regime, the quality of housekeeping was rapidly deteriorating. Guests who previously had never filled out e-mail comment cards were now taking the time to respond, and the feedback wasn't pretty. The basics weren't being attended to. Guests complained that toilets weren't clean, the carpets weren't completely vacuumed, and the rooms often smelled of mildew and mold. The only training new employees were provided was on-the-job baptism by fire, as Carla would not "waste" resources on training. Rob thought to himself that this could be the biggest challenge he'd have to handle. And he also knew that it was one of the first things he needed to address.

It was almost time for lunch, so Joe decided to give Rob a taste of The Harper's restaurant. By now the word had spread throughout the hotel that the new boss was on the grounds and it was in everyone's interest to be on their best behavior. The hostess was polite enough, seating Joe and Rob quickly, but without much conversation. Rob noticed that she didn't make eye contact with them. The menus were dropped at the table and conversation about the morning ensued.

"Do you honestly believe this place is salvageable?" asked Joe.

Rob paused for a moment, looked up from his menu, and said, "I don't know. It feels pretty overwhelming and we're only a half-day in. I've never seen anything like this, to this extent, this magnitude. I do believe, however, that it's worth my best effort and I'm committed to the work ahead. I'm here, and not looking back. There's nothing I can do about the past, but there are a ton of things I can do to ensure the future is different. I'm confident that I can help change the course of this place. The only question is whether I can do it quickly enough for the board—oh, and whether I'll have the support and resources necessary to make the changes this situation will require."

Both Rob and Joe opted for salads. After all, it's tough to mess up a salad. Rob continued to notice that most of the waitstaff were just going through the motions, moving without a bounce in their step. He never had to worry about any of the waitstaff in Chicago. Folks were proud to be part of a world-class organization, they loved living in Chicago, and every waitstaff member took pleasure in engaging the customers in conversation. He would figure it out, but at the North Carolina property he was pretty sure it was either a DNA thing (the employees just didn't have it in them), or an environmental issue.

The afternoon looked, sounded, and felt just like the morning. Rob remembered that he has not yet had a Red Bull, so he took a short break to visit with Cat in the gift shop. He saw it as an opportunity for a double pick-me-up. A dose of caffeine and a dose of Cat! This second visit to the gift shop gave Cat the opportunity to engage Rob in deeper conversation, and he welcomed the interaction. Cat wanted to know everything about him, about his family, and about his plans for the property. Rob learned she was a great listener, and he mentally made note of the fact that as he was talking to her, she was one hundred percent "*there*," despite everything else going on around her. The only time she looked away from Rob was when the occasional customer came in. Cat quickly and effectively redirected her energy to the customer, and Rob was impressed with what he saw. He decided to quietly slip out the back of the gift shop, letting Cat take care of her customers.

Around six o'clock that evening, Joe decided they had seen enough for the first day. Joe also figured that both he and Rob had spent enough time together, so they agreed to part ways for dinner. Joe suggested a few places near Rob's apartment, all within walking distance. As Rob pulled out of the parking lot, he took one last glimpse of the hotel in his rear-view mirror and wondered how a place so beautiful on the outside could be so ugly on the inside.

7. Choose to be Positive

As Rob slumped into Sebastian's on Main, he was greeted by a young hostess named Alissa. What initially struck Rob most was her smile—Alissa simply lit up the room. It was just what the doctor had ordered for Rob, at the end of a day that seemed so overwhelming and hopeless. Alissa welcomed him to Sebastian's and made it a point to notice the fatigue in his face and in his voice. "Looks like you've had a rough day! We'll do everything we can to make your evening stress-free and enjoyable."

With that, Alissa guided Rob to a table near the fireplace, handed him the menu, never taking her focus off him while she was in his presence. Despite the fact that the place was packed and she was incredibly busy, Alissa remained calm, professional, and warm. While Rob's experiences with restaurant staff ranged from excellent to abysmal, he sensed immediately a heightened level of energy and positivity running throughout Sebastian's. His thoughts drifted to the task ahead of him with his hotel, and the contrast couldn't have been more extreme. After finishing his dinner and having experienced a wonderful consistency of approach, attitude, and gracious hospitality throughout the evening, Rob decided he had to figure out the "Sebastian's Secret." He asked to meet the owner, and his waiter gladly went and found proprietor Bill Sebastian.

"Tell me, how do you do it?" asked Rob, after meeting and shaking Bill's hand. "I'm new to town and I was blown away by the fact that from the moment I walked in, I was greeted and treated like family."

Bill sat down across from Rob, took off his work apron, and began to share. "I learned a long time ago that you could have great food at a fair price in a good location, but if you don't *select* the right people—*talent*—you are doomed. We don't hire, we *select*. I literally get forty to fifty folks a month who come through those doors wanting to work here. We don't pay any more than the guy down the street; people just *want* to work here. I could hire any warm body but I don't. Like most businesses, ours is all about relationships. People do business with people they like. If your people are negative, indifferent, or just going through the motions simply to collect a paycheck, customers sense that and eventually stop coming.

> *Like most businesses, ours is all about relationships. People do business with people they like.*

Most of the time they won't tell you why, they'll just stop coming around and before you know it, your place is empty. Here at Sebastian's, I hire for attitude. I can train anybody to wait tables or to be a hostess. I want someone who cares, who is fully engaged at work, someone who wants to be here serving people. And I'll tell you this—it's no secret, but the way to get your staff to treat customers like family is to treat your staff like family. Our staff is treated with dignity, respect, and love. They know we truly care about them, as a person, not simply as an employee. And they extend that same care to our customers. I'm convinced that the key to customer satisfaction is employee satisfaction. And the key to employee satisfaction is having a management team that creates a culture of respect, love, and dignity.

"So I hire shift and department managers with great attitudes. I look for passion, energy, enthusiasm, drive, and commitment. You can't fake that stuff. I believe attitude is a choice, and it's not circumstantial. Every single day you wake up, you have a choice. It's either going to be a good day or a bad day. It's up to you. There are folks in this world who will try to suck the life out of you, and while we must love and rise above them, we don't have to hire them! Energy Vampires need not apply here. I want folks who infuse this place with energy, with positivity. If you come in and we see that your attitude is bringing everybody else down—either co-workers or customers—you are gone. And I don't care how good you are or how long you have been here. It sounds harsh, but it's my livelihood—it's how I put food on my table, make my mortgage payment, and how, someday, I'll be able to afford to send my kids to college. I take the right attitude seriously and am not willing to put all of that at risk by keeping someone with a bad attitude on my staff."

> *Every single day you wake up, you have a choice. It's either going to be a good day or a bad day. It's up to you.*

Rob could sense Bill's passion and conviction—it came through his pores! Here was a guy who modeled a standard of excellence for his staff. One of his secrets was that he chose his attitude daily and expected those who worked for him to do the same.

"One last thing I'll share with you, lest you think I'm Pollyanna," Bill said, thoughtfully. "I know people are gonna have bad days. I know stuff happens in life outside of these four walls that get people down. I know people have challenging personal issues that come their way. But as I tell my folks, you simply can't let customers in on your bad day. I'd rather you go home and take the night off than come in here and go off on a customer because you're having a bad day. Everyone understands that expectation because I communicate it with them before I select them to work here."

With that, Bill excused himself, but not before thanking Rob for coming in and experiencing Sebastian's. Rob watched as Bill made eye contact with every member of the staff as he passed, acknowledging them and calling them by name. Sebastian's *was* a family, and it was obvious that Bill walked the talk.

On the short drive back to his apartment, Rob began to process what he had seen and heard, and realized that his experience at Sebastian's had energized him, despite the fatigue he was fighting, and the overwhelming nature of what lay ahead. He had been searching for an answer as to where to start with The Harper. He now knew.

He would start with the people.

8. Make Their Day

Rob rolled over in bed and looked at the clock on the nightstand, daring it to flip over to five o'clock. It seemed like he had JUST fallen asleep. He clearly hadn't drifted off to sleep last night, nor would he qualify the minuscule amount of sleep he managed to snag as restful. Both of those states would have required a clear mind and the weight of the world on someone else's shoulders. Still, he managed to extract himself from the bed and lace up his running shoes, then headed out the door and into the streets for his energizing and mind-clearing morning ritual. During the run, he thought through the day ahead and what needed to be done. He'd be back at The Harper for day number two, and decided he'd start by gathering his management staff for a discussion about people. Changes were required, and he knew deep down that some of those on his direct report staff would be part of the necessary changes.

Rob wrapped up his run in front of the YMCA and decided to complete the session with a short core workout. One of the

perks of being a Y member in Chicago was that he he could
use the local facility as a guest until he transferred his mem-
bership. As he walked through the lobby toward the front
desk, a staff member approached him with a small white
hand towel, a bottle of water, and a warm smile.

"You must be new to these parts! I'm Jill, and from the
looks of it, you could use a towel to wipe away that hard-
earned sweat and some water to rehydrate," said Jill Golden,
with a big smile. (Rob later learned she was the Guest Services manager.) "Welcome to our Y! How about a high-five?"

Holy Cow that felt GOOD, thought Rob. *She doesn't even
know me and she greets me like that? It's almost as if she knew
I was coming. . . .*

"Thanks Jill!" Rob responded. "That was an awesome
welcome and very thoughtful of you. In fact, I gotta tell you,
even though the day is young, you just made mine!" As Jill
walked with Rob to the front desk, he said, "Nobody has ever
greeted me like that after a run. What a great practice. Do
you do that for everybody?"

"I don't, Rob, because not everybody who walks through
those doors has just come back from a run; but for those who
do, I try to greet them like I greeted you. And for those who
don't, I try to think of something special I could do to make
their day! Regarding the towel and water, I came up with the
idea a few years ago. I'd see people walk through here with
sweat dripping off their foreheads and their faces bright red,
and it just seemed like something small I could do to help
bring them back to life," Jill said, laughing. "And a funny thing
happened along the way: I actually began to look forward to
getting up every morning and coming to work! I couldn't wait
to come in and discover new ways to make people's days. It
gave me purpose. Honestly, I don't even like to take my breaks
because I don't want to miss anyone. I know some people

come in here in the midst of a rough day, and many people are carrying burdens we can't see, so if only for a few moments I can give them a boost, bring a smile to their face, and make their day, I'm on it. And you know, most of what I do doesn't cost anything other than an investment of time."

"I can see how energizing others totally fuels you!" exclaimed Rob. "I'm so impressed by the fact that you come in every day looking for ways to create special moments and build relationships. I would venture to guess that there is a huge ripple effect that you don't even see—the smile as they leave is probably the tip of the iceberg. I bet they in turn do something nice for someone else—maybe they leave here and go hug their wife or assist a co-worker without being asked. Who knows, but it will impact someone else. I love it!"

"Thank you for noticing, Rob. If there is anything else I can do for you or get for you while you are my guest here, please do not hesitate to ask. Have a great workout!" And with that, Jill bounced off to anticipate the needs of another Y member, and Rob headed upstairs to work his core, still shaking his head and wishing he had half of Jill's energy and enthusiasm.

Energized by his run and inspired by Jill, Rob rolled into The Harper with renewed optimism. If he had thought about the challenge ahead with any logic whatsoever, he'd be packing it in right now. It was only day two, but already he could see that the attitudes and culture of complacency  and indifference would be hard to break through. Once again, neither Janice nor Ben was at the front desk. He walked up and waited—and to his dismay he saw the dreaded sign posted beside a silver "hospitality" bell.

He cringed. His first reaction was to take the bell and chuck it across the hotel lobby, but he remembered that cooler heads prevailed. He took a deep breath, then tapped the bell. Several times, loudly. It didn't take long for Janice to come out from the office with a look on her face that said, "This better be important!"

"Can somebody please explain this?" questioned Rob. "Can someone give me one good reason why we'd have one of these things anywhere on our property? Are we that short staffed that we can't have somebody full time at our counter greeting and checking in guests?"

Janice muttered a combination stutter/mumbled response, something like, "Well, that's the way it was done when I was hired and I never questioned it. ..." Rob repeated the question. In response, Janice called to Ben and attempted to deflect the question his way. "Ben, do *you* know why we have the bell?"

Ben was a bit better prepared to answer the question, but he could tell Rob wasn't buying it. "Here's the deal folks—we are in the HOSPITALITY business. We are HOSTS. We are here for our guests, 24/7. First impressions are lasting impressions. If the first experience and impression of our hotel is an impersonal interaction with a desk bell, that's not good. In fact, in this day and age, that's unacceptable. I'm sorry, but while you both are working here, clocked in, there is nothing more important than being at this front desk—present and available—for each and every guest."

Both Janice and Ben seemed shocked that they were somehow being blamed for a practice they had inherited. It was clear neither wanted to take responsibility. So Rob was direct. "I'm headed on a tour of the hotel, but I should be back around noon. And when I return, we're going to spend some quality time together. I have some things I want to share about my expectations for your positions. I understand I owe it to you both to allow you the opportunity to hear and apply these expectations, and I apologize in advance for voicing my frustration. While I have heard that you both have been in the hospitality business for some time and know the reservation system like the back of your hand, my concern is for the 'softer'

> *First impressions are lasting impressions.*

stuff—attitude, presence, tone, passion, and commitment." While Ben nodded his head (perhaps more out of fear for his job than out of agreement), the eye-roll Janice gave Rob was unmistakable. Rob had seen it many times before when challenging someone who clearly didn't want to be challenged. Instead of engaging further, Rob moved on, knowing his first personnel decision had just been made.

9. Invest in You

Rob spent the rest of the morning walking the grounds and meeting one-on-one with Joe. He shared some of his initial impressions with him, none that seemed to shock the industry veteran. Joe, who was taking off after lunch, reminded Rob that he'd be back in a week to check in; that is, assuming Rob was still here.

"Before I head out, there's someone I'd like you to meet," suggested Joe. He owns and operates a local bookstore here in town. I think you'll find the conversation interesting at the very least, and perhaps there's a book or two he could recommend for some 'light' reading at night after the long days I know you have ahead."

Joe and Rob walked the few blocks from The Harper to the bookstore, and when they got there, Rob immediately noticed a dapper, distinguished older gentlemen awaiting their arrival at the front door. "I'd like you to meet Mr. Gary Blake," said Joe.

"Well a fine, wonderful welcome to you both!" exclaimed Gary. "Joe, it's always a pleasure to see you."

Turning to Rob, and extending the same firm handshake he had just given to Joe, Gary said, "I understand you are new to these parts. It is my hope that you experience the Southern hospitality for which we are well known. And I for one will do everything in my power to make sure you feel right at home in my store. Please, please come inside."

With that, Gary led both Rob and Joe inside, through and around the amazing yet seemingly unorganized collection of books on the shelves. "I know what you're thinking," suggested Gary, with a twinkle in his bright blue eyes. "How can there be any rhyme or reason to this place; it just looks like books, books, and more books galore. Well I can assure you that *I* know where every book is and I am always here. So if you have any titles in mind, just ask. In addition to the thousands of titles I carry, I think I have a copy of every book ever published about North Carolina. But first, please, have a seat."

Gary led Rob and Joe to a back corner that was set up for reading. Large beanbag chairs, couches, and recliners filled the area and despite the fact that it was mid-day, the corner was empty. "I asked my team to help keep this space available for just us, even if it's only for fifteen or twenty minutes. There's so much going on in this world, sometimes you just have to slow down, carve out the time and space, and take a life-break."

"So you are probably wondering why I brought you here," Joe commented to Rob.

"Well, the thought did cross my mind," admitted Rob. "I like books but truthfully, since graduating from college, I haven't spent much time reading anything save for maybe *Sports Illustrated* and the occasional Sunday newspaper. I just don't have the time."

"You mean you don't *make* the time," challenged Gary. "I don't mean to be disrespectful, but we all have the same number of hours in each day. We just make different choices about how we spend those hours. Over the years, I have learned that investing time each day stimulating my mind— learning, gaining knowledge, expanding my mind, and developing an understanding and appreciation for things to which I otherwise would have never been exposed—makes me a more valuable person to those around me. I hear you are a runner. You somehow find the time to run, right? It's the same concept, just mental development instead of physical development. Now granted, reading has become a passion for me and I've made it my livelihood, but I want to let you in on a little secret: *Leaders are readers.*

"Harry Truman once said, 'Not all readers are leaders, but all leaders are readers,' and I couldn't agree more. Every great leader I have ever read about throughout history has been a voracious reader. These men and women realized at some point in their lives that books hold the key to exceptional leadership. Many great books have been written and are still being written by leaders from all walks of life, books that hold the keys to unlocking the leadership capacity and capability within all of us. Yet, too many people assume learning stops when they graduate from high school or college. Too many people count on others to provide development opportunities instead of taking responsibility for developing themselves. Or they simply don't make the time to invest in themselves. Let me ask you a question. You fly a bit, right? When you get on a plane and the flight crew goes over the safety instructions and features of the plane, they explain what you are to do in the event of a loss of cabin pressure as the oxygen mask comes down from the ceiling. Let me ask you, Rob, whom do they say to put the mask on first?"

"Me, I guess," replied Rob.

"Why do you think that is, Rob?" asked Gary.

"Well, I'm assuming that if something happened to you while putting on your child's mask, for example, you'd be of no help to anyone else?"

"Bingo!" said Gary. "I've experienced a lot in my long life, but perhaps the most important life lesson I've learned is that you've got to make time to grow YOU—spiritually, mentally, emotionally, and physically. It seems selfish and counterintuitive, but the bottom line is this: invest in you and there's more of you to give away. Let me see if I can give you another example. Bill and Melinda Gates have *billions*, right? Did you know they give away an extraordinary amount of money, too? Do you know why they do? It's because they are philanthropic and care about people, but they give away money because they *can*. The more they make the more they can give away. It's the same with anything else in life. Learn more through reading books and you'll be able to share more knowledge and pass along those learnings to help mentor someone else. At the end of our lives, we'll know it's not been about us, but about who we've been for others. By enriching our minds through books, we can become better versions of ourselves for others. You'll be a better leader. A better husband and father. You'll be a better friend. And you might just avoid some of the mistakes I made in business years ago as a young leader, before I was introduced to the practice of reading books as part of my personal and professional development."

> *The bottom line is this: invest in you and there's more of you to give away.*

Rob sat there, taking it all in, mesmerized by the wisdom and philosophies he was absorbing. It all made sense, and it was clear Gary *lived* the stuff he was sharing. Rob could tell their time was drawing to a close, and his stomach was reminding him that they still hadn't eaten lunch.

"Thank you so much for your gift of time, Mr. Blake," said Rob. "I want to be a great leader, and I know I don't have all of the answers. It's apparent that this bookstore and these books are filled with answers to some of life's greatest challenges; and from a business perspective, I'm thinking just about any issue we may face has been thought through before and written about. Can you suggest a book to start?"

A deep smile broadened across Gary's face. "Somehow I anticipated that question. So, here you go." And with that he reached back to the table behind his couch and retrieved a small, gift-wrapped package.

"This my gift to you, my investment in you, my belief in you. I don't want you to open this now but I do want you to think about what I've shared, let it sink in, and when you have some quiet time this evening, open this up. All I ask is that you do two things: read it, and then pay it forward. Find someone to give the book to; someone who you've discovered needs the message held within. Oh, and a third request: don't stop at this one. Keep reading. Come back to my bookstore; Learning is a lifelong pursuit."

> By enriching our minds through books, we can become better versions of ourselves for others.

"What can I say but, again, thank you," Rob responded. "I promise to read the book, I promise to pay it forward, and I'll commit to you that this won't be the last book I read." With that, Gary accompanied them to the front door and wished them a fine rest of their day.

When Rob's feet touched the sidewalk, he was suddenly and harshly reminded of the overwhelming challenges awaiting him that had temporarily receded while he was with Gary and time seemed to stand still. Rob thanked Joe for the introduction. He couldn't wait to see what book Gary had selected, and he anticipated that somehow he'd be able to put the lessons learned from them to good use at The Harper. Lord knows he needed every bit of help he could summon.

With Joe on his way back to his home office in Phoenix, Rob returned to the hotel and began mentally preparing for an afternoon of challenges. The first thing he decided to do was make a change at the front desk. Janice would have to go. By all accounts, and based upon what he had already witnessed, she was just going through the motions, collecting a paycheck, putting in her time, but contributing nothing and adding no measurable value for the guests. He recalled the eye roll, her response to his challenge about being present and available, and thought back to what Bill Sebastian had told him about talent: in any service industry, hire for attitude, train for aptitude. The front desk was such a crucial post and with Janet behind the counter, it currently reflected poorly upon the reputation of The Harper. Rob also understood that letting Janice go would send a message to others who might be coasting. Indifference and mediocre performance would no longer be acceptable at The Harper.

Janice's departure was no surprise to most staff members. As is the case after most terminations, the staff wondered what took so long. Rob took Ben aside after Janice left and explained his rationale. He shared that he'd not only be finding a replacement for Janice, eventually he would also be adding an extra front desk attendant. That way they would be able to ensure that at all times, all needs and guest requirements could be handled with little to no wait.

He remembered something Emily had told him after attending a Tom Peters seminar—a key message from the session: "You can't shrink yourself to greatness." Remaining short staffed would be the quickest way to the bottom. He told Ben that he had arranged for some one-on-one shadowing time at the YMCA with Jill Golden, and that he would gladly pay Ben for his time. Rob considered it an investment he believed would pay dividends for both The Harper and for Ben personally. He ended their conversation by confirming that he believed in Ben and saw something in him that suggested he was capable of much more, and that the opportunity to work in an environment free of the influence of Janice might just be what he needed most.

Rob spent the rest of the afternoon walking the floors and listening. While he hadn't read many books, he had heard stories of great leaders and tried to apply some of those lessons learned along the way. He recalled a story told about Sam Walton and his leadership style during his time starting up and running Wal-Mart. Sam spent very little time in the home office of Bentonville, Arkansas. Not because he didn't like it there, but because he knew the home office was insulated from the action. He'd often fly into towns to visit his stores and to meet the folks doing the real work, day in and day out. Upon his arrival, he'd gather employees, maybe say a few words of introduction, and thank them for the good work done on behalf of Wal-Mart and its customers. Then, he'd pull out a pen and a pad of paper and say, "I know what I know, now tell me what you know." And he'd stop talking. And listen. And learn. Sam believed that the answers to most of Wal-Mart's issues and challenges were held by those closest to the customer, on the floor. The problem, he believed, was that leaders in many companies never got out of their offices and walked around.

Rob's time walking around was proving invaluable. He carried a pad and a pen, and took pages of notes. He spent fifteen to twenty minutes with each employee, asking a series of questions he knew would help him address the challenge ahead.

1. If you were running this hotel, what's the first thing you'd do?
2. Do you feel "in the loop" in terms of communication?
3. Do you feel there's collaboration across teams here?
4. How do you know if you are doing a good job?
5. Are you proud to be an employee of The Harper?
6. Would you recommend this hotel as a workplace of choice to friends?
7. What three words would you use to describe the work environment?

Rob figured that with honest answers to these seven questions, he'd have a pretty good idea what the current state was and how big the gap was between where it was to his desired state, his vision. He knew a thing or two about vision as a former college athlete, and he knew that it took hard work, dedication, and discipline to make visions a reality. The world of business was no different. His vision for The Harper was simple: people would make reservations months in advance because the place was so popular. The hotel would be filled to capacity because word-of-mouth generated from guests experiences was so compelling that people couldn't wait to experience The Harper.

At the end of his second day, Rob sat alone on a lobby couch with his thoughts, his pad, and the book he'd soon be unwrapping. He was tired, but at the same time energized by the thought that perhaps, just perhaps, he could make a difference and save this hotel.

10. Pursue Excellence

On her way out the door, Cat noticed Rob and couldn't help but stop and check in with the new manager. "So what do you think so far? I could make an educated guess, but I'd love to hear your initial impressions," said Cat.

"Hello, Cat! Hmm. . . . Let me first qualify things by saying that you have been *the* breath of fresh air around here, and if I had one hundred Catherine's working here, we'd be setting occupancy records. So that is my challenge: to stay positive and focus on the good things going on while addressing those things I can impact. We'll get there for sure, and I recognize that it will not be easy, but somebody once told me that nothing worth achieving ever comes easy."

"Well, I believe in you," assured Cat. "I have a feel for people, and I get the sense that you have what it takes to lead us back to excellence. Everyone wants to be part of a great organization, and I don't plan on going anywhere anytime soon because I know where we can go and I want to be part of what is possible."

"Thanks for the vote of confidence, Cat," replied Rob. "I know that we can't get there without you. So please keep the faith!"

Cat hesitated before leaving. "Just a thought, not sure what plans you may have for this evening, but I have an extra ticket to the Vienna Boys Choir tonight at the civic center—they are performing *Edelweiss*. With summer only a couple of months away, it may be just the perfect diversion from your professional challenges. The conductor is a close friend, and the tickets include a meet and greet post-concert. What do you say?"

The name "edelweiss," and its association with love and summer caused an ache of loneliness and longing for Rob. He missed his wife and children. The thought of summer and that beloved mountain flower—considered the ultimate love potion—was inspiring. "I would LOVE to join you! I have never been, but it's on my bucket list. That would be a *very* cool thing to do tonight. What time shall I join you?"

"The show starts at seven thirty, so let's meet outside the civic center at seven and we'll head in from there. I can tell you that it is something special to behold. I also have a feeling you'll really enjoy seeing such an amazing team of musicians work together to produce an incredibly beautiful experience. It's more than just music—it's a feeling that the music produces. . . . I could go on forever, but you'll just have to experience it for yourself. I'm so excited to be able to share this "gift" with you!"

In order to be on time or early, Rob opted for a quick bite to eat downtown, and after parking, made his way over to the civic center to meet Cat. He couldn't believe how fortunate he was to have such an opportunity. He had always wanted to see the Choir, and had heard wonderful things about *Edelweiss*. The combination of those two great things in one night was almost too good to be true.

Cat was there on time as promised. She was beaming as she handed Rob his ticket. She had already seen the performance, but to attend with someone who had never been, who had always wanted to experience such an evening—well, it didn't get any better than this. In her many years, she had come to discover that life was about *doing*, not *having*. Experiences, not material possessions, created memories. And the greatest experiences were always shared.

After the two found their way to their seats and settled in for the sold-out show, Rob felt compelled to share a bit of the story he associated with *Edelweiss* and its connection with his family. After sharing that edelweiss reminded him of the promise of summer and of being united with his wife and children, the lights went down and the performance began. It was as if somehow Rob had been transported out of this mountain community for three hours, taken away from the troubles, worries, and challenges he was facing at The Harper, and the ache for his family. The show was simply magical. It was obvious that every young man in the choir brought their very best that evening. The powerful, triumphant rendition would surely have made its composers proud. Rob had done some pretty cool things in his life, but this was different and powerful in ways he'd never imagined.

After the concert had come to a close and the audience acknowledged the collective brilliance of the Choir, Cat and Rob made their way toward center stage and with their two backstage passes visible, they were led by security to a meet-and-greet waiting room that was already filled with family, friends, and invited guests. Cat had grown up with the Choir's conductor and had stayed in touch with him over the years. "He has always been one of the hardest working and driven guys I know," explained Cat. She shared that Lars had a dream of one day conducting a great choir, and he stayed focused on that vision throughout his life. He lived intentionally, even at a young age, and took advantage of every opportunity he had to learn from the best and to see the best perform around the world. He sacrificed other things along the way—putting off what he wanted in the moment in exchange for what he most wanted out of life. His dedication and commitment to personal excellence was recognized upon graduation from Julliard and he was given many opportunities to gain invaluable experience over the years. Experiences that ultimately led to this opportunity of a lifetime.

Still wiping the sweat from his face, conductor Lars Johansson made his way into the room and gave a general welcome. He immediately noticed Cat, and sought her out first.

"Well, what did you think my dear friend?" asked Lars as he warmly embraced his childhood friend.

"Brilliant! Simply brilliant!" exclaimed Cat. "But I must admit that I didn't expect anything less than amazing this evening. And once again neither you nor your choir disappointed. Lars, I'd like you to meet Rob, a friend of mine and, as I have shared, the manager of the hotel where I work."

"It's an honor to meet you, Mr. Johansson," said Rob, clearly honored to be shaking the slender and expressive hand of the great conductor.

"The honor is all mine, Rob," replied Lars. "I only have a few minutes but Cat texted me earlier this evening and said that you'd be here tonight and asked if I could share some thoughts with you as I understand you have quite the challenge in front of you.

"First, let me say that I have been in your shoes before. I've inherited choirs over my career in need of so many different things. I was told numerous times that I shouldn't put too much effort into turning things around because it was a 'lost cause.' I basically was brought in to make a quick decision as to whether or not the most immediate season was salvageable. In every case, I told the folks hiring me that there isn't anything I do in life with less than one hundred percent effort. I see every challenge as an opportunity. One of my favorite quotes earlier in my career came from Walter Bagehot, who once said, "The greatest pleasure in life is doing what people say you cannot do." So I use challenges to fuel me, realizing that if I could do something with what others viewed as hopeless, I could establish both a name for myself and a reputation for excellence. I saw every opportunity as an audition for something greater down the line. I never expected anything more of others than I was willing to do and give myself. I've made it clear to every member of every choir I've ever led that I had high expectations of them, and that I would hold them to a high standard, but the standard to which I hold myself would be even higher.

"And a funny thing happened along the way. I expected the best in the people I led and directed and most of them gave me their best. These kids here tonight, they are no different than anyone else. They want to be affirmed, encouraged, respected, dignified, and loved, but deep down they also want to be pushed, to be challenged to give their best and be their best. They all want to be part of something greater than themselves. It's my role to help them become the very best versions of themselves, while also teaching that they are but one part, one element, of a team. I let them know that for a team to succeed, every single member must commit to excellence. All it takes is one musician to give less than his best, and the entire experience is compromised.

"Ultimately, my choirs have come to realize that what drives and inspires them is not so much me as their own willingness and desire to bring their best to every practice and every concert—not just for themselves, but also for their fellow choirmates. And I have since learned that Mr. Bagehot was wrong: the greatest pleasure in life is actually seeing someone you have mentored achieve something they once thought impossible.

"And Rob, it's no different in the hospitality industry. You need to select the best talent, and you need to share your vision of excellence with them—what it will look and feel like when they've achieved it! The standing ovations we receive each night never get old. My kids want to be part of excellence, they want to bring audiences to their feet, and they want to provide concert attendees with an experience that they will never forget. You see, I believe that what we do isn't simply music. Yes, we sing and are generally accompanied by an amazing orchestra playing beautifully behind us. But what we are creating is an *experience,* if only for a few hours, that allows people to feel emotions they otherwise may not have access to. I've come to learn that people need what we can provide, and the truth is that they are willing to pay just about anything for that opportunity."

> *The greatest pleasure in life is actually seeing someone you have mentored achieve something they once thought impossible.*

With some final words of encouragement, Lars graciously excused himself and moved on to others waiting to greet him. Rob let Lars' wise counsel sink in as he and Cat made their way back out through the civic center and into the cool, dark night. Rob thanked Cat for the evening, for the extraordinary experience, for the introduction, but most importantly, for caring enough to remain on staff and to be an important part of a shared vision.

11. Be Remarkable

Rob couldn't sleep. He drifted off for a few hours, but rest proved elusive. His mind was on overload and thoughts of what he had to do and how he'd go about doing it kept sleep at bay. After a few hours of tossing and turning, he decided to get up and go for a run. It was only four o'clock, but he could think of no better way to settle his mind and organize his thoughts. He knew he'd pay for it mid-afternoon, but for now he was wide awake. He didn't expect to find anyone out at that hour, but a mile in he could hear footsteps behind him and figured it had to be a fellow runner. The runner was quickly gaining on him so he slowed down to speed up the inevitable. The "pass" happened but his pride kicked in, so Rob decided to see if he could return the favor. It was dark but this much he knew: she was young, fast, and energized by the music on her iPod. He took off after her but soon realized that she understood that it was "game on." His repeated attempts to close the gap failed but he kept her in sight and soon noticed that she was headed back to the same finish he was, within yards of his apartment complex. With one final kick, he pushed through the last quarter mile and finished behind her. She was already into her post-run stretching when he came to a stop and assured her that he was not a stalker.

"Nice job out there! I run that route quite often and rarely see anybody else, especially at this hour, let alone anyone who tears up a run like that. You were really smoking," commented Rob, who also took the opportunity to introduce himself.

"Thanks! I'm Debi. Are you new to town or just here on business?"

"Actually, a bit of both," responded Rob. "Just came in from Chicago a few days ago, and I gotta tell you I'm still getting used to this altitude. And the hills. We have nothing like this in the Windy City, so I guess we kinda got a false sense of fitness. Here it's like I'm starting over. My lungs and my legs burn, big time. I'm not having fun quite yet."

"Give it time," assured Debi. "I have been here several years and, like anything new, the adjustment took time. But I stayed at it and never allowed myself to get discouraged. The way I see it, the hills and the altitude are challenges that can only serve to make you stronger. The hard is what makes it all good. Anyone can run flats. But training at altitude on these mountainous roads and trails has prepared me for some of the toughest races I've entered. So instead of thinking about them as a negative, I embrace the tough."

Rob was intrigued. Here was this gal with such energy and this incredibly positive perspective on things about which he'd often catch himself complaining: hills, altitude, the hour of the day, the weather, you name it. He quickly realized she was a unique combination of tenacity, positive attitude, and discipline. He figured there was a reason the two had connected that morning.

"If you have fifteen minutes, I'd love to buy you a coffee," offered Rob. "I'm sure you know there's a Starbuck's right across the street."

"Are you kidding? I have stock in that place," laughed Debi. "In fact, I *work* at that place. I've been a barista there for about as long as I've lived here in this beautiful mountain community. I love my job and the people who come in. I'm never a customer there but today, for you, I will make an exception," Debi said, smiling.

Rob and Debi walked in, and of course everyone there knew Debi and greeted her as if she was family. It didn't surprise Rob, knowing that people didn't just come to Starbucks for the coffee—in fact, he actually preferred the coffee at Dunkin' Donuts. But nothing could beat the experience of Starbucks.[2] Combine great coffee, a great vibe, really cool people, and a unique ambience, and you have an unbeatable recipe for success. Rob took the opportunity to share with Debi some of what he was up against. She responded that she was aware of the size of the challenge he had inherited because many of her customers had been on the receiving end of The Harper's poor service at some point over the last couple of years.

"I think I know one of the problems you're facing, without even stepping foot in that place," offered Debi. "Now correct me if I'm wrong, but based on what I've heard, you have some employees who don't really want to be there. Employees who are quite literally going through the motions, surviving Monday, getting over hump day, working for the weekend, and collecting a paycheck. It's a job for them, not a cause. For those people who are doing the bare minimum, it wouldn't matter if you increased their pay a buck an hour. It's not about the money. You need folks who want to be there, who want to serve, who come in every day wanting to stand out and be remarkable. Being remarkable means looking and working outside the boundaries of your position description. I come in every day *intentionally* seeking opportunities to do things people don't expect. I try to go for the "WOW" factor. Anybody can take an order, make a coffee, and make change on a sale. I want to make a difference. So I strive to go above and beyond and become so valuable to this coffee shop that they could replace my position but they could never replace *me*. I go out of my way for people; I want them leaving this Starbuck's a better person for having run into me. My goal is to be the best barista Starbuck's has ever employed."

Rob was impressed. Debi seemed to exude a passion and a zest for life that went far beyond her ability to kick his butt on the road. She had purpose—something that got her out of bed in the morning. Her runs went much more quickly because she couldn't wait to get into work and see what the day had in store for her.

"Let me try to explain through a story, Rob. For us, it's all about delivering legendary service. That's shorthand for being relational with people, making a connection that goes way beyond a simple business transaction, intentionally engaging our guests in conversation and then seeking out extra efforts to serve them. There was this lady who came in every day and ordered the same thing: a cinnamon Dolce Latte. She wasn't the friendliest or the most conversational guest—in fact, most days she'd never look at me when she ordered. I kept being me, treating her with dignity and respect, trying each day to pick up any cues I could from her in an

My goal is to be the best barista Starbuck's has ever employed.

effort to personalize my service to her. I found out her name and always greeted her accordingly, but one day I decided I'd hand-make a card for her with some words of encouragement and hand it to her with her latte. I knew about when she'd come in every day so I had it ready when she walked in and ordered. She handed me her money and I handed her the latte and the card. She was obviously caught off guard and it was clear she didn't know how to react. I simply told her that I hoped she had a great day and wanted to let her know how much I appreciated seeing her every day. She took her latte and her card, unopened, and left.

"The next day she returned, same time, same order, but without the look of indifference she had worn on all previous visits. She had this ear-to-ear smile and made a point to thank me for taking the time to write such affirming words on what she described as 'a beautifully hand-made card.' She shared that nobody had ever done anything like that for her, and she was so impressed that someone who made her latte would go and do something like that for her. She explained that she had been going through a really difficult divorce and she felt the weight of the world on her shoulders. She was scared, tired, angry, and admittedly not the nicest person to be around. She had questioned her worth as a human being and kept coming up with the same answer: she was a failure and maybe life was no longer worth living. The card and my words had encouraged her and uplifted her in a time of need."

As Rob listened, he could hear in Debi's voice, in the words she didn't say, that she had received as much, if not more, from that act of kindness and from being "remarkable" as her guest. By going above and beyond, by doing that which was not expected, by operating far outside the boundaries of her job description, she had made a difference in the life of another human being when that person perhaps needed it most.

Debi ended her story by sharing that each day brings opportunities to be remarkable in so many ways. It was the little things she noticed she could do for people, and the little things added up. She talked about the ripple effect as well; some call it the "Pay it Forward" principle. She had no idea how many people were affected in some positive way by her small, daily gestures, but she did know one thing for sure: people kept coming back and business was booming.

Rob thanked Debi for her time, and for sharing her story and her insights. By reaching out, she'd made a difference in Rob's day, too. Debi thanked Rob for the latte, and they both agreed to meet again for a run—and Debi joked that the next time it would be at Rob's pace.

12. Be Present

While Rob's arrival at the hotel on day three was unannounced, the staff now anticipated him and it was becoming clear to them that there were different expectations with regard to how they were to go about doing what they do while on the job. Several staff members had already submitted resignations, making Rob's job a little easier as he went through the process of determining who were the "keepers" and who were the "sleepers." Sleepers were folks who slept-walked through their days. These were staff who were rarely "present" with people, those who felt it was far more important to respond to a personal text message than respond to or anticipate a guest's request. That morning, Rob had scheduled some time to meet with Robbin Worthington, a dear friend who had re-located to the area from Chicago several years ago. Robbin had heard that Rob was in town and, as always, had this instinctive way of knowing that he could use her advice and counsel. Robbin had served as an unofficial mentor to Rob in his early days with The Harper, but the two had drifted apart with her move and his rise through the ranks in Chicago.

Robbin arrived, as expected, a few minutes prior to their ten o'clock appointment. She was always a little early for any meeting, formal or informal, personal or professional. She believed that showing up, on time, for a time previously committed, was a sign of respect for the other person and his or her time. She simply couldn't fathom being late, yet knew people who were *always* late for things. While she was an easy going, non-judgmental person, it was one of the things that grinded on her most in life. If you say you're going do something or be somewhere, do it.

"So, what do you think of our beautiful town?" Robbin asked Rob. "It has been a few days now, surely you've formed an opinion."

"I love it here!" Rob replied. "I love everything about it—the mountains, the people, the energy, the downtown. This is one very cool place, I can see why it is consistently ranked one of the top travel and retirement destinations. Having said that, it would be even cooler if I could play as much as I have to work."

"You GET to work Rob," half-chided Robbin, with a chuckle. And from past experience, he knew she was calling him on something he'd forgotten. The "have to" vs. the "get to" component of life.[3] One simple change in our perspective can make every difference in the way we go about life, and who we are while we're doing what we do.

"So, tell me honestly, how are things going Rob?" inquired Robbin. "I have an inkling regarding what you are up against; the grapevine around these parts remains alive and well. I'd prefer to hear it straight from the source, however. Or shall I say, the savior?"

Rob laughed. "Wow, word does travel fast! And yes, you could say that I'm feeling the weight of this situation sitting squarely on my shoulders. I am not sure if I'm the right guy for this assignment but I have come to terms with the fact that it's an opportunity, something I "get" to do. I just needed that reminder, so thank you. It's funny, but that life lesson is one that continues to make a big difference, year after year."

"Well, I'm glad I've made an impact on your life, and I want you to know that I will always be here for you. I'm not a "catch and release" kind of friend. I'm here for the duration," said Robbin. "We've got one hour together, and I'm all ears."

For the next sixty minutes, Rob talked and Robbin listened. She gave him the gift of her undivided attention. She was wholly present, there in the moment with him, not distracted by her iPhone or any other device. Rob recalled their very first meeting years ago, and the thing that struck him most about her then remained true today: she was "there." Being there, being present with people, means stopping what you are doing when someone comes into your office to talk. It means not "switch-tasking" by texting when someone is trying to talk to you. It requires the discipline of being focused on the moment at hand, like there is nothing else going on around you but your time with that person.

One simple change in our perspective can make every difference in the way we go about life, and who we are while we're doing what we do.

When Rob was finished, Robbin played back to him what she had heard. She agreed that he had a people problem that was affecting the culture. And behind people problems within most organizations lies a deeper root cause: a lack of leadership. She shared that many CEOs seek her advice and counsel on how best to address declining customer satisfaction—revenues and market-share losses typically follow dips in customer satisfaction. Despite the fact that most don't want to hear it, CEOs come to realize with Robbin's support and encouragement that the issue is often employee satisfaction. Unhappy employees are simply not capable of taking care of customers, at least not in a sustainable way. The best companies she had ever worked with were led by visionary, compassionate, humble, bright leaders who selected the very best employees, and then treated them with dignity, respect, and love. In turn, the staff treated customers the same way. Companies like Southwest Airlines, Zappos, Amazon, Nordstrom, The Ritz-Carlton, and Mayo Clinic all "got" it. It was a simple concept, but much more difficult to apply.

Rob listened carefully, even though he already knew the answers to many of the questions he posed to Robbin. She was an invaluable sounding board, and he knew he'd need her particular brand of advice and counsel for the next several months if he stood any chance of saving this place. Rob knew there was no such thing as a solo effort. Anything worthwhile ever accomplished, personally or professionally, was made possible through the collective efforts of family, friends, mentors, and co-workers. As their time drew to a close, Rob asked Robbin if she had twenty hours a week she was willing to contribute to the cause. He'd pay her well for her time, and if it proved too much, she could cut back on the agreed-upon time investment.

> *Rob knew there was no such thing as a solo effort.*

Robbin thanked him for the invitation and said that she was very interested, but needed an evening to think it through before making a formal commitment. Rob felt good about the probability that Robbin would join the team, if only for a short time.

As Robbin got up to leave, she gave Rob a hug and looked him in the eyes. "You can do this. I believe in you." It was exactly what he needed to hear. While he had confidence in his own abilities, he also knew that the encouragement of others fueled him. It didn't take much, just a bit of affirmation, knowing someone had faith in your capabilities. He respected Robbin and knew how valuable her time was—the fact that she'd even consider helping him spoke volumes about their friendship and her support as his mentor.

Energized by his time with Robbin, Rob made his rounds on the grounds of the property, meeting with people, taking more notes, and making decisions about the things he knew he needed to address. One of those "things" would be to select several new department heads, building a direct-report leadership team that would share both his values and those of The Harper. There was so much to do, so many things to consider, and so little time left.

13. Be Intentional

*R*ob's thoughts were interrupted by the buzz of his cell phone; it was Emily, checking in to see how his first few days had gone.

"So, you are still there?" joked Emily. "Folks here at corporate have been placing over/under bets on the number of days it will take for you to tell us you want that return flight to Chicago."

"Funny! But I don't give up that easily," Rob replied, laughing. He really appreciated her humor during this especially stressful time. "While I will admit that I hadn't anticipated the depth and breadth of the problems here, I'm far from throwing in the towel. I believe things are salvageable, but I also know that I'm going to need help."

Rob shared his plan to bring Robbin on board in a consulting role. He also indicated that he would need more staff to cover guest peak periods. He talked about the keepers and the sleepers, but before he could share any more Emily gently interrupted him.

"Rob, it sounds like you are already knee-deep into a process and a plan, which is great. I'm here to lend my help in any way I can. I see my role as one of providing the necessary resources you need, removing any barriers or obstacles to your success, and encouraging you through this process. I know it all seems overwhelming, but can I give you some advice and counsel?"

"Of course," Rob replied, "I'm all ears."

"And please take this as it's intended. We gave you this opportunity, fully recognizing that you did not have all of the tools necessary to succeed. We won't let you fail, but we also intended this to be a learning experience for us all. It sounds like you are seeking the support and guidance of others, like Robbin, and I'm sure that by now you know this turnaround isn't something you can accomplish solely on your own."

> *Inherently, people desire to be part of something greater than themselves.*

"Understood and thank you for saying that. I still feel tremendous pressure to succeed here but I do realize that I'm just one part of the solution," Rob replied. "I know that I am not in this alone."

"Well, you are the most vital and critical component," Emily affirmed. "Your role here is to provide a vision the staff can embrace and own for themselves. People want to know where you are taking them. Inherently, people desire to be part of something greater than themselves. Your number one role is to help establish the purpose that will drive their passion for what they do each and every day. Every morning when their alarm clocks go off, they have a choice. They can either stay in bed, or get up and get going. If they have a greater purpose—something to which to contribute their time, effort, and energy—a *cause*—you will see it reflected in their attitude and demeanor.

"So having said that, you must first establish a vision and then support it with a mission. The mission will fuel their purpose. What is it that people will come in and do—every single day—to the very best of their ability that, over time, will bridge The Harper experience from where it is now to the vision you've championed?"

Rob thought for a moment and then replied, "My vision for this place is no different than the vision we had in Chicago. Occupancy at one hundred percent, people making reservations months in advance, and compelling word-of-mouth recommendations from guests who were blown away by our inimitable service."

"How many people working here know that?" challenged Emily. "I know you are only a few days in, but you'll need to communicate your vision to folks and consistently share with your team members what it will look like and feel like when that vision becomes a reality. How will they benefit and why should they buy into your vision? You don't need to answer that question just yet, but give it some thought because you need buy-in. And every time you add somebody new to the staff, you'll need to ensure that they not only support your vision and mission, but that it's something that excites them, as well. And I know this probably goes without saying, but you'll also need to think of ways to reward and recognize folks along the way. It's not good enough to simply wait until the vision is realized. People need to be encouraged throughout the process, especially as strides are being made and quantifiable results begin coming to fruition.

"But first things first," Emily continued. "One of the things I do before taking on an assignment of this magnitude is to develop an initial, written ninety-day plan. It helps me maintain the discipline of intentionality. I have learned that either we run life, or life runs us. Without a written plan, you end up spending the vast majority of your time on what I'll call "walk-in business," or, gravitating to whoever is screaming the loudest for your attention. And a daily plan only becomes tangible and actionable if you have planned out beyond the day. You need to ask and answer for yourself what your week and month looks like and what it is that you *expect* to accomplish over the course of that period of time. I start with the end in mind and work backwards to the present, establishing a timeline and goals for what I hope to achieve."

Rob sensed a personal story coming. Emily had accomplished many things in her life, both personally and professionally. She was someone who had achieved a wonderful sense of balance: she was a mother to three beautiful daughters, and had gone back to school for her MBA part-time at nights while working her way up the corporate ladder. She was on a number of boards, volunteering her time within her community, and she had competed in a number of marathons over the years. For her, too, running was a passion. Rob hadn't yet built up either the courage or the mileage to tackle the marathon distance, but it remained a dream and a goal of his.

"I know you are a runner, as well, so I'll give you a running analogy, Rob. I'm aware that someday you'd like to take on the marathon distance. I understand this town hosts a marathon in September. You wouldn't just show up on race day in September and expect to be able to run the distance. It wouldn't be entirely impossible, but it wouldn't be pretty. It would be painful, there would be parts you'd have to walk, and you'd pay the price afterwards for your lack of preparation.

"So instead, you find someone who has done a number of marathons. You seek input on developing a twelve-week plan that includes a progression of mileage, building up over the course of that period with daily runs, attention to nutrition and recovery, and a proper taper period three weeks out. With your plan in place, and knowing your vision (crossing the finish line 26.2 miles later), each day you have a mission that pretty much can't be compromised. You do that which gets you one step closer to realizing your vision. Your daily runs, cross-training, core work, diet, sleep, and those weekend long runs aren't always fun or easy, but they are vital to your success on race day.

"Some days you won't want to go out and do the work but you must. Over the course of the twelve weeks, you'll notice changes in your body's ability to adapt to an increased load. You will most likely lose weight, you'll get faster and more efficient, and you will develop the mental strength required to push through the distance when the day arrives because you've paid your dues. But essentially, each day you are prioritizing and preparing for a desired future state, closing the gap between your current state and your future state.

"Work assignments are no different. You have six months to turn this place around, but you can't start the work five months in and expect miracles. There's no such thing as an overnight success. You need a plan, a prioritized list of activities that must be accomplished to see your vision become a reality. You need the advice, counsel, and support of others. There will be sacrifices, tough decisions to be made, long days, and some sleepless nights. But as I have shared with so many people, there are no shortcuts to any place worth going. Nothing worthwhile is ever achieved without challenges and sacrifice.

"Crossing the finish line of a marathon is overwhelming, mentally, emotionally, and physically. Yet, it's not the day itself or those 26.2 miles you covered—it's about the twelve weeks of training, sacrifice, and dedication. It's the journey, the process of becoming a marathoner that is so valuable. A journey that culminates when you cross the finish line. This will be the case here, as well. You will turn this place around; it won't be easy, but it will be worthwhile. And you will use this experience to build upon as you are offered future assignments. With every assignment taken on and seen through to the end, you'll have take-aways and invaluable lessons learned that you'll always have to apply going forward.

"But it all starts with living a life of intention. Each day—on both a personal and a professional front—you will have decisions to make regarding how you will spend the limited number of minutes and hours. We all get 1,440 minutes to spend each and every day, any way we wish to spend them. We can waste them, we can spend them on things that don't and won't matter years from now, or we can treat them like gold, ensuring we maximize their use in the pursuit of those things that really matter.

"And now, I'll step down off my soap-box," Emily said with a sigh and a slight smile. "I'm sorry to have gone into such detail about being intentional but, as you can tell, I'm passionate about the topic. I see far too many people making excuses instead of making the time and a plan."

"No, I truly get it, Emily," responded Rob. "That's the one thing I haven't yet done here. I need to spend one day removed from the operational aspects of running this place. After having spent several days here being overwhelmed while gaining an awareness and a perspective on what needs to be done, I am now ready to establish a plan. I am ready to prioritize those actions that will be required, and identify the resources necessary to make my vision a reality. It's easier said than done, but it must be done, and I intend to do it."

Emily wished Rob the best of luck and let him know, again, that she was only a phone call away for advice, or just a flight away should he need her on-site. Rob knew that he could lean on her, but he also realized that this was his opportunity to own, and if he called Emily to the property, it would effectively be admitting he couldn't handle the assignment. Besides, she had other things to worry about and manage. He realized outside support would be vital to his success, so he was going to build a powerful leadership team to ensure that Emily didn't need to become personally vested or involved in the turnaround.

14. Be Kind and Thoughtful

*T*he conversation with Emily still fresh in his mind, Rob found a quiet conference room in the hotel, opened his day planner, and began writing. He'd spend the next eight hours in that same room, taking short breaks as needed but being very intentional and focused on the list of actions required, resources needed, and timing required for all that would need to take place. At the end of the day, tired but satisfied, Rob had completed a ninety-day plan that was ready to be reviewed with Emily.

As he was getting ready to leave, Rob remembered a couple of things he hadn't gotten to that day: he had forgotten to eat lunch, and he had yet to unwrap the book Gary had given him the day before. He packed his laptop and day planner, grabbed his cell phone off the table, and decided that tonight, instead of going out to dinner, he'd have dinner in. He wasn't much of a cook, which made him think about his wife's amazing cooking skills and her gift for setting a beautiful and inviting table, and gave him even more to miss about her. Even though he talked with her each evening last thing before bed, when they shared the day's highs and lows in the undisturbed quiet, it never seemed like enough. Reluctantly shaking himself out of his thoughts of his beloved, he told himself that frozen pizza would have to do, given the fact that it was already after seven and he was just leaving the hotel. Both Joe and Emily had mentioned good things about a health-food grocery store near his apartment, so he decided to give it a try.

It was dark when Rob pulled into Whole Foods, and he was tired, hungry, and on edge. He generally maintained a positive attitude and tried to be happy, but tonight—after having spent an intense day thinking about how much work lay ahead of him and how little time he had for himself or his family—he felt big waves of doubt and uncertainty wash over him. He turned the engine off and sat there, wondering what these waves were about. The plan was coming together, he had gotten some great advice and counsel, he had the support of Joe and Emily, and he believed he'd get the resources necessary to make the changes required. Rob continued to sit quietly in the darkness of his car, trusting that the cause would surface. Sure enough, understanding began to dawn on him and he realized that perhaps the biggest challenge he faced was perhaps beyond his control. Perceptions die hard. He could make every change possible to the staff, the environment, the culture—he could even bring in a new chef and change the menu at the restaurant. But there would still be a lingering negative perception of The Harper that had been formed over years by the collective set of individual experiences guests had had with the hotel staff. How to change perceptions, long after the hard work had been done to remove anyone or anything having to do with how those perceptions were formed—*that* was the million-dollar question. He could advertise, he could buy television spots and internet ad space, and he could even invite travel agents and guide publication staff to The Harper to see firsthand the changes that he and his team had brought about. He realized that he wasn't going to solve the issue tonight, but the "perception is reality" concern wasn't going away. His stomach growls reminded him that, for now, it was time for dinner.

Rob had been to several Whole Foods stores before, but never this one. After he figured out where the frozen-food section was, he made a beeline for the pizzas. He loved Paul Newman's Organic Pizza. Not only because it was good, healthy pizza, but buying it helped to support and promote a great cause with 100% of the proceeds going to Newman's Own Foundation.[4] The box read, "Paul Newman and Newman's Own Foundation have given over $300 million to thousands of charities since 1982." Rob let that sink in for a moment. He wondered about the extent to

> *Newman's Own products were "good stuff," but the company did not exist to make a profit. It existed to make a difference.*

which The Harper had any involvement within the community, from a philanthropic standpoint. He was a firm believer that it takes a community—that business does not exist in a bubble, that what is good for the community is also good for business. And the purpose of being in business must rise above simply making profits. Making a profit was necessary to remain in business, but there must be some greater good to which a business contributes. It must play a role within the community, to some necessary end, to promote some greater good. Newman's Own products were "good stuff," but the company did not exist to make a profit. It existed to make a difference. He recalled The Harper's involvement in Chicago with the local food pantry and the homeless shelter. Both causes were near and dear to Emily's heart, and it reminded him that he hadn't noticed (at least not yet) the extent to which The Harper property in North Carolina supported any community causes. His assumption was that the hotel was in self-preservation mode, which meant any consideration for anything or anyone else was non-existent.

Rob got to the check-out counter, opting for the express lane with his one item, and reached into his coat for his wallet. A feeling of panic began to well up inside him as he realized his wallet was not where he thought it was. He mentally backtracked to his time in the conference room and immediately realized he had left his wallet on the conference room table, having pulled it out that afternoon to buy a Red Bull at the gift shop. It was a good fifteen minutes back to the hotel property, a thirty-minute round trip if he still intended to have frozen pizza for dinner. As the options rushed through his mind, the cashier had already figured out what was playing out and asked Rob how she could help.

"Gosh, I'm really sorry!" Rob said, with an embarrassed look. "I seem to have left my wallet at work. I can't believe this. It's been a very long day and in my haste to leave the office, I forgot to grab my wallet. I will put the pizza back and come back later."

As he was turning away from the register, Rob noticed the cashier's name tag at about the same time she introduced herself. "My name is Jodee. Welcome to town! I'm so sorry you forgot your wallet, I've done that before and it's SO frustrating. Oh, and a little embarrassing for sure. But I'll tell you what, you look like a trust-worthy soul so go ahead and take the pizza. I'll pay for it out of my own wallet, and you can stop back in anytime to pay me back. No worries. I'm here every day from noon to seven-thirty, same aisle, same name tag, same smile. Please, you look tired and hungry; your day has been long enough. And I know something about long days so I can relate."

"I can't ask you to do that," Rob insisted.

"You didn't ask—I offered," Jodee said with a smile. "And quite frankly, since I offered, it would be rude of you as a newcomer to these parts to turn down my Southern hospitality. And something tells me you have it within you to pay the gesture forward somehow, some way, for somebody else. So please, take the pizza. I've got you covered."

With that, Jodee rang up the sale and bagged Rob's dinner. He didn't know what to say, aside from "thank you," as she handed him the receipt and the pizza.

A thought occurred to Rob, and he asked Jodee, "You mentioned that you start work at noon. Do you work somewhere else in the morning?"

"No, I attend classes part-time. I'm putting myself through school, so when I told you I know something about long days I wasn't kidding. After work, I head home and study. This isn't my dream job, but for now it is paying the bills and funding my education. I fully expect at some point to be working in my field of study, which is sales and marketing. I view this job as an audition for other opportunities that may come my way; you just never know who might walk in here. I love meeting new people! Working here allows me the opportunity to hone my relationship skills because—trust me—you meet all types here. ... Okay, maybe that sounded bad, and I'm not suggesting you are one of those "types," Jodee laughed. "But truthfully, you should get psychology credits for working in any service industry. People come in here with all sorts of stuff going on in their lives and I just try to make the moment or two that they spend with me time they won't forget. I figure the world is a cold, ruthless place for a lot of folks. If I can shower them with kindness and do something nice for someone once in a while, I will. I see every customer as an opportunity, not an obligation. It totally changes your perspective when you see people that way, and you choose to serve them with kindness and thoughtfulness. You probably know what I'm talking about. Do you travel much?"

"Well, not really," answered Rob, "but I have traveled my share and do know my way around the service industry. I do know what you're talking about. It's rare to find those qualities in people within either the service or the hospitality industry. Kindness, thoughtfulness, patience, consideration, empathy ... I could go on. It's just so rare. That's why a simple act like you paying for my pizza feels so significant. It's because it isn't something that I have come to expect in life. Most times, I'd simply leave the pizza with the cashier or take it back to

> *I see every customer as an opportunity, not an obligation.*

the freezer myself. Oh, and that's *after* I get the eye-roll and the deep sigh of frustration and disgust from the cashier. Neither of us wins in that scenario. In fact, it's a lose-lose: I'm embarrassed and the cashier is upset. My experience is neither positive nor memorable. I will probably come back to the store but I certainly won't have a story to tell someone else about my experience."

"True that," replied Jodee. "Well listen, my shift is up and I need to cash out, but it was so very nice meeting you. Please come back and visit us here at Whole Foods any time and, seriously, there is no rush on paying me back."

Rob smiled at that and said, "I will be back tomorrow. In the meantime, if you're open to the idea, I'd be honored to look over your resume. Here is my business card; my email address is at the bottom. When you take a break from studying tonight, feel free to shoot me an email."

"I will, and thank you," Jodee replied. "Have a wonderful evening, and enjoy your pizza!"

With that exchange, Jodee closed her register and Rob left smiling, once again energized by an interaction with someone he'd just met. He had come into the store tired, hungry, and a bit jaded, but he was leaving with renewed faith in the human race and an idea for The Harper.

15. Live Your Values

*R*ob's pizza tasted better than expected. Perhaps it was the fact that he was so hungry, but it also could be because he had just been on the receiving end of a very kind gesture, which felt good in the midst of an often not-so-kind world. He remembered the book he had received from Gary remained in his backpack, and decided to use the time prior to packing it in for the evening to unwrap the gift and read the note he'd received from Gary in this morning's mail.

Gary had taken the time to hand-write a note on thick vellum stationery. Rob carefully broke the seal, opened the envelope, and began to read.

Dear Rob,

It was a pleasure meeting you. There's so much I want to share with you but all in due time. I'm sure we'll have the opportunity to get together again and would hope that you take me up on my offer to be your official book recommender.

Never forget that leaders are readers. In my long life, I have come to know that there are many folks out there who have figured out things and then written about them so that I can benefit from their collective experience, knowledge, and insight. Books are gifts. Please accept the book from me with the hope that it enhances how you lead and, perhaps most importantly, who you are as a human being. This book is one of my all-time favorites, a story about a man who I believe to have been the single greatest leader of men my generation has known.

Remember, as well, that it is nearly impossible to read books and come away unchanged. And change is good. Who you were yesterday may not be enough for what will be expected of you tomorrow. I hope you will discover that books can give you a fighting chance at staying relevant, both professionally and personally. It was the man whom this book is about who once said, "Five years from now, you're the same person except for the books you've read and the people you've met."

I'm already a better man for having met you my new friend!

Gary

Rob took a few moments to let Gary's words sink in before unwrapping the book. Inside he found Steve Jamison's, *Wooden: A Lifetime of Observations and Reflections On and Off the Court*. He had heard so much about Coach Wooden over the years, and knew that he had led his UCLA Men's basketball team to ten NCAA championships, winning 88 consecutive games (still a men's NCAA basketball record). Most importantly, however, Rob knew that Coach Wooden was a man who lived his life both on and off the court in a way that was deeply aligned with his ideals and principles. He lived his values.[5]

Despite the fact that it had already been a very long day, Rob opened the book, began reading, and couldn't put it down. It was late and he'd be up early for his morning run, but he somehow knew that the lessons inside this gift would shed some light—and perhaps a path—for the task ahead, and that now was when he needed those lessons. He thought back as he was reading to some of the adventure races he'd competed in, and how it would have been impossible to race at night without the headlamp worn by each team member. The lamp made visible the course ahead, and helped ensure his teammates minimized any risk of injury that could have resulted from unseen obstacles encountered during the race. The insights, lessons, and principles Jamison wrote about in *Wooden* would serve Rob in similar fashion, helping to guide his thoughts, words, and actions as he faced the challenges ahead.

What impressed Rob most about Coach Wooden was the fact that he walked the talk. He had high standards for his players, yet he never held anyone to a standard he wasn't willing to maintain or exceed himself. Win or lose, he remained the same man with the same faith and the same consistent behaviors. His life was a testament to his teaching, and for

him, success wasn't defined or determined by winning or losing, but rather by giving your best and being your best. Winning without adhering to values was losing. Coach Wooden
lived his life, regardless of the circumstances he encountered,
consistently and true to those beliefs he held sacred.

Rob had seen examples in his own career of leaders who
would assure others that their values aligned with those of the
company, only to default to their own set of values—values
that were very different and often in conflict with the corporate values. Especially when times got tough, when business
was down, competition got aggressive, or when problems
multiplied. Rob had learned that anyone can be positive,
calm, patient, focused, honest, committed, enthusiastic, and
confident when times are good. But few people can maintain those values when a storm hits. He'd visited other hotel
properties over the years in an effort to identify best practice,
and he could generally tell within the first several minutes of
a visit whether the values within were lived or merely words
on a framed print. His gold standard was The Ritz-Carlton,
where the motto that guided employee thoughts, words, and
deeds is: *We are ladies and gentlemen serving ladies and gentlemen.* Rob still had the credo card given to him during his
tour of the Naples, Florida, property.

> **The Ritz-Carlton Hotel** is a place where the genuine
> care and comfort of our guests is our highest mission.
>
> We pledge to provide the finest personal service
> and facilities for our guests who will always enjoy
> a warm, relaxed, yet refined ambience.
>
> The **Ritz-Carlton** experience enlivens the
> senses, instills well-being, and fulfills even the
> unexpressed wishes and needs of our guests.[6]

So maybe The Harper would never be The Ritz, but why not strive to be the best, why not adopt similar philosophies and practices? Why not hire people who are genuinely passionate, positive, relational, professional, competent, and capable? Why not select managers who model the way for their folks, managers who treat staff as fellow team members, not just direct reports. Why not work hard to create an environment where people feel empowered to do whatever is necessary to take care of the guests, one where phrases like, "It's not my job," or, "Let me check with my manager," are never uttered? An environment where people feel respected, dignified, and loved. A place where people LOVE coming to work, because they GET to serve guests and—as a result of thinking and acting outside of the boundaries of their position descriptions—they have a renewed sense of purpose as they go about their job of anticipating the needs of guests. Where the ladies and gentlemen who work the property are recognized and rewarded for going above and beyond, to the point that going above and beyond becomes the standard, not the exception to the rule.

> *Rob had learned that anyone can be positive, calm, patient, focused, honest, committed, enthusiastic, and confident when times were good. But few people could maintain those values when a storm hit.*

It was close to midnight, but Rob's mind was racing again and sleep would prove elusive. He sat on his bed with the finished book on his nightstand and smiled, knowing that there would be a tremendous ripple effect upon the lives of others as the result of this simple gift from Gary, and the profound and lasting legacy of the life of Coach John Wooden.

16. Putting the Pieces into Place

No alarm clock was necessary this morning. Despite only five hours of sleep, Rob awoke energized and hopeful. Pieces, he knew, don't fall into place on their own, they must be intentionally and purposefully *put* into place by someone who has the conviction and commitment to see things through to the end. He now not only more fully understood what he was up against, he also understood why he had been tapped to lead the turnaround, and who he now needed to involve to help make his vision a reality. He also knew that he needed to share that vision with those he brought on board. They needed to buy in to where he was taking them, and they needed to "own" their piece of the solution. This would not be a one-man show. But it would start today, and it would be led by one man who had been inspired by many.

Rob's run this morning was the best of his jaunts in his new town thus far. His lungs now acclimated to the altitude and his legs more comfortable with the climbs, he ripped off a strong six-mile loop, hardly breaking a sweat, which was aided by the cold, crisp morning. He raced through a quick shower, grabbed a bowl of cereal, and headed to The Harper.

Enroute to the hotel, Rob called Joe. He knew that he could use some on-site counsel and support next week as he began to build the foundation for The Harper's comeback. Rob shared his thoughts with Joe, his plan, and the name he'd come up with for the turn-around effort: Project No Reservations (PNR). The name was the perfect double entendre to describe both the current and desired state of The Harper. For Rob and his team to succeed, they would have to convince guests who, for some very good reasons, had significant reservations about booking a room and staying at the property. If they were successful, the phone would eventually be ringing off the hook with people calling because they had no reservations whatsoever about staying at The Harper Hotel, or recommending the place to others. Compelling word of mouth would spread as guest experiences became legendary, and a new legacy of service took shape.

Joe agreed to join Rob for the communication roll-out to the staff on Monday morning. Joe would fly in from Phoenix on Sunday so he could spend the better part of the afternoon with Rob reviewing the plan in detail. Rob was ready, but he also knew there were several things he needed to do before Sunday's meeting with Joe.

⚜

As he pulled up to the hotel, his cell phone rang; it was Robbin. She was a woman of her word and was calling back right on time, as promised. Rob held his breath, hoping her response would be positive.

"I've thought and prayed about this, Rob," Robbin began. "As you well know, this is no easy assignment. But I was channel surfing last night and came across one of my favorite scenes from one of my all-time favorite movies, *A League of Their Own*. Coach Jimmy Dugan, played by Tom Hanks, is trying to convince one of his players, Dottie Hinson, played by Geena Davis, to stay on the team instead of heading back home to Oregon. She says to him, 'It (baseball) just got too hard.' To which he replies, "It's supposed to be hard. If it wasn't hard, everyone would do it. The hard … is what makes it great."

"That one line has become a personal mantra for me. The way I see it, you can go through life taking the easy, comfortable route, but you'll never experience the deep satisfaction and joy that comes from accomplishing great things. And to accomplish great things you must be willing to do 'hard.' I'm calling to tell you that I look forward to doing the "hard" with you because I know that together, we can turn this thing around."

What great news! With Robbin on board, Rob felt even more convicted about the road ahead and what he needed to do next. It had been less than a week since his arrival, but it had seemed like well over a month. Robbin's first project would be to pull together a guest council, a combination of folks who had stayed at the hotel before, and those who had not. The goal would be to collect constructive feedback and best practice suggestions from people who considered themselves either regular business travelers or recreational vacationers. Rob knew that too many businesses—regardless of their industry—tried to guess or predict the needs of their clients/patients/guests/customers. Why was it such a novel concept to gather those folks together and *ask* them what they desired? To find out what it would take for them to come back? How could we do a better job taking care of the things that they most cared about? Is it possible that many businesses were actually afraid of what their customers might tell them? Rob knew that the good ones wanted to get better, that "Good to Great"[7] took a combination of welcoming transparency and maintaining thick skin. Customer feedback is a gift, not a gavel.

Rob's next move was to let Carla go. Emily had once told him that firing someone was perhaps the most difficult thing a manager must do, and that it never gets easy no matter the circumstances or the number of times. She told him that if it ever did get easy, it would be time to move on and do something different, because that would mean that you've lost your heart as a leader. A leader must lead with both her head and her heart. Rob gathered Carla's team and shared the news. As he had anticipated, there were visible smiles of relief and it was clear that as far as they were concerned, the end to Carla's reign of terror was long overdue. Rob recalled his first tour of the rooms and halls earlier that week and felt the deep contrast between the mood then and the mood now. This was a good start. The natural question came up regarding Carla's replacement.

Customer feedback is a gift, not a gavel.

"At this moment, I don't have anybody in mind," Rob admitted, "but for the time-being should you need anything, please come directly to me." Rob proceeded to share with the staff his vision for The Harper; he wanted to be sure everyone understood that while the road ahead wouldn't be easy, eventually it would be rewarding. He shared that this team was perhaps the most vital and critically important group on the grounds. He wanted them to know how important their jobs were, to him, and to The Harper.

"You need to remember that there is no such thing as an unimportant job. We all have a role to play here, and if this vision of mine—that now becomes *ours*—has any chance of becoming a reality, it will take all of us collectively, and each one of us individually. Guest opinions are formed, quite literally, one experience at a time. And all it takes is one bad experience and an opinion is formed, a perception is cemented, and a reputation is established. I'm committed to each and every one of you, but you need to be committed to each other. You are a team and, as individuals working together to help provide the best possible environment for our guests, it should not be about what *I* want—it should be about what *they* want. I will help ensure this environment is one in which you feel respected, dignified, and loved. In return, I hope that you would extend those same values to your fellow team members and to our guests."

Rob could tell that nobody was completely buying (yet) what he was selling. The longer people live or work under regimes of oppression, the longer it takes for them to be convinced that the new paradigm shift is real. Rob realized that with employees, just as with his daughters, they'd wait to see if his walk matched his talk. This situation reminded him of one of his favorite sayings by Ralph Waldo Emerson: *What you do speaks so loudly that I cannot hear what you say.*

> *A leader must lead with both her head and her heart.*

Those he'd be bringing on board to lead the change he hoped to see must first and foremost walk the talk. Model the way. Live the values. He didn't necessarily care how much supervisory experience within the hospitality industry someone had, but he did care how much heart the person had. A heart for people. A heart ready and willing to be of service to both staff and guests.

⚜

Rob's next visit was to the gift shop, where he found Cat assisting a customer who was obviously enamored with Cat's unique approach. Rob must have looked "official" because on his way out, the customer made a point to tell Rob how impressed he was with Cat's presence and relationship skills. "I travel the world and I can tell you, people like her are rare," insisted the gentlemen. "I'm not sure what you pay her, but I'll tell you this: you need to replicate her around here to stand any chance of being relevant five months or five years from now."

"I appreciate the feedback," Rob responded, "and I'd have to agree with you. My job would be significantly easier if I had a hotel full of team members like Cat. She is a gem, and clearly whatever we pay her isn't enough. But I'd venture to guess that what she does—and who she is while she's doing what she's doing—is not about the money, but about her love of serving people."

Rob made sure his comments were made within earshot of Cat, even though he knew many talented people shied away from overt praise. He didn't know how much longer she planned on being with The Harper, but he wanted to make sure she knew how much she was appreciated and valued.

"How goes your morning, Cat?" Rob asked.

"Too quiet," Cat replied. "I prefer it busier. I know you are working to improve things, but there was a time when this place was packed with guests and I didn't even have time for a bathroom break. It sounds funny, but I long for those days again.

I'm at my best when I'm with people, and we need more people. The days go by so much more quickly, but most importantly, I feel like I'm fulfilling my purpose when I'm helping others."

Rob said, "I understand, and you have my commitment that six months from now this place will be packed with people. I have a vision, and I want to share it with you because the hotel needs you in order to help make this vision a reality. My vision is that our phones will be ringing off the hook with people calling to make reservations. My vision is a lobby chock full of people enjoying the grand fireplace and bar. My vision is a team of hotel staff committed to the daily pursuit of excellence and the anticipation of guest needs, where we are intentionally going about exceeding the expectations of those guests each and every day. My vision is a day filled with guest comments like the one I just heard—not just for you, but for everyone on staff!"

> I'd venture to guess that what she does—and who she is while she's doing what she's doing—is not about the money, but about her love of serving people.

"Wow!" Cat exclaimed. "That would be a very cool thing to see played out here. Is it doable?"

Rob smiled at Cat's comment, then said, "Yes. I believe so. Having said that, there is no doubt it will require significant work for sure. Know that I'm wide open to your suggestions, Cat. And I have a favor to ask. I'd love for you to help develop and deliver a new employee orientation program with me. We can discuss the details later, but you "get it," and I couldn't imagine our new folks getting a more positive first impression and a clear understanding of what we are trying to do, than from you. Think it through, and let me know if you have any questions. Because we're on a tight timeline, if you could let me know your decision sometime tomorrow, that would be great. I'm off now to visit with more folks but as always, I welcome any other advice and counsel you'd be willing to offer. I don't have all of the answers, but I am smart enough to know who I can turn to for assistance and I also recognize it's my job to pull it all together and drive the change. Thank you for being a shining beacon for what we will become!"

With that, Rob retreated to the quiet of his office to make a phone call. It was a long shot, but he figured it was worth a try. He pulled up his new contact list and found the name and number that had been foremost on his mind after gaining Robbin's commitment to join the PNR leadership team. He dialed the number, knowing that it was Friday and Jodee most likely was enjoying her only day off from both school and work.

"Jodee, this is Rob from The Harper. I'm not sure if you remember me, but ..." and before Rob could get out another word, Jodee jumped in.

"Of course I remember you! How could I forget? You were the guy who tried to get a free pizza from my store the other night using the old, "I forgot my wallet excuse," she said, laughing.

"Okay, I must admit, I would have preferred to meet under different circumstances, but I'm a believer that things happen for a reason and, looking back, I'm actually glad I left my wallet at work. It gave us a chance to meet. You turned an obligation into an opportunity, and now I have one for you," Rob said, grinning to himself.

"I'm intrigued," Jodee responded.

"When we met, I neglected to tell you *where* I work or *what* I do. I am the General Manager for The Harper Hotel here in town, and I need to make some radical changes if my vision for the place is to become a reality. You shared with me that you eventually want to get into sales and marketing, and that you love working with people. I need someone to work the afternoon and early evening shifts as my 'Director of First Impressions,' someone to work the lobby area and greet arriving guests. First impressions are lasting impressions and I think you make an *amazing* first impression. You have a smile that lights up any room, and you are incredibly relational."

"But I've never worked in the hospitality industry. I don't remember the last time I even *stayed* at a hotel! Seriously, there's got to be more qualified candidates than me in this town, ..." Jodee said, her voice trailing off.

"I can *teach* you the ins and outs of the hotel industry," Rob affirmed, "but I can't teach what you've already got on the inside: passion, energy, positivity, your light. That and the fact that you seem to intuitively think out of the box, unconstrained by conventional norms. The average cashier would have made me put the pizza back. You took a different approach, you trusted me, and you made a lasting and memorable impression. Not just personally, but for Whole Foods. That's what I can't teach, so I intend to hire for that trait."

Jodee was quiet for a moment while she took this in. Then she said, Thank you. Thank you for noticing those qualities in me, and for thinking of me for this position. It sounds like this job would offer valuable experience, training, and the opportunity to hone skills better suited to sales and marketing than my current position allows. Don't get me wrong, I love what I do, but I guess I am ready for the next step."

Rob smiled. "Excellent! Now, let's talk compensation. I have a pretty good idea what you currently are making. How does a twenty-five percent increase sound? I know it's not just about the money for you, but you have school to pay for and The Harper wants to help you realize your dream of getting your degree. If everything works out, I'd love to have you come on board full time after graduation."

Jodee seemed very excited by the offer and asked for two weeks to give Whole Foods notice. Rob thanked her for saying "yes!" so quickly and said that he would e-mail her an offer letter, and looked forward to having her join the team.

Rob's next call was to Bill, the restaurant proprietor he met at Sebastian's. He knew The Harper's restaurant required significant changes, and they needed to happen now. Corporate had loaned him a head chef from another property for the short term, but he needed his own exceptional waitstaff. Knowing Bill interviewed folks all of the time and probably turned away some highly qualified candidates, Rob reached out. Bill was pleased to hear from him, and generously shared that he had hired several seasoned staff for a series of lavish dinners he'd been hired to host by a local company. The dinners were first class and the company was more than willing to pay top dollar for top talent. They would be hosting the last dinner in a week and after that, he'd be letting those people go. He said they were wonderful folks, in fact one in particular would be toughest to lose. She had come in and transformed the ambiance in the short time she worked there. Her name was Alissa, and as much as he wanted to keep her, he couldn't rationalize letting someone go who had more seniority. And, Alissa had fully understood the temporary nature of the hire.

Rob couldn't believe his good fortune—this was the one and the same Alissa whose smile lit up both the room and Rob's heart. He didn't hesitate confirming that he'd love to have her on board. Bill shared a few more names and backgrounds, and Rob made plans to make calls and set up interviews.

His next hire was to replace Carla. He knew that the cleaning staff represented the foundation of The Harper. It simply didn't matter how many happy, positive, energetic people he had working the property, if the basics weren't covered—a clean, warm, and welcoming room—nothing else mattered. Execution of the fundamentals, the basics, no matter what the business, is a non-negotiable. Rob remembered how much pride the staff at the Chicago property took in each and every room. Each floor had a small team assigned to cover the level, and a healthy competition grew between teams as they sought daily perfection. There was a framed print hanging in their break room—almost sacrilegious in Bears' territory—featuring a quote by legendary Green Bay Packer head coach Vince Lombardi:

> *Perfection is not attainable, but if we*
> *chase perfection we can catch excellence.*

As he considered his options, he noticed a text message come up on his cell from Emily. She was checking in and asking him to call when he had a minute.

"How goes the battle?" Emily answered when she picked up Rob's call.

"I'm getting there. One by one, I'm putting the pieces into place. I know what I want to do and whom I want on board. We'll get there; I'm beyond hopeful now ... if I can just figure out who I can get to replace Carla."

"Well, funny you mention that," responded Emily. "You remember Caroline, our high potential new hire from about eighteen months ago in Chicago? She's ready for her next assignment, and quite frankly I don't have a natural next move open for her in Chicago. She's never led an entire

room-cleaning staff for our property, but she's a quick study—
and besides, you need strong leadership, not necessarily the
best room attendant. She mentioned a willingness to relocate,
and while I haven't yet approached her about North Carolina,
I have a feeling she would go."

Rob couldn't believe his good fortune. "I do remember
her! She's got some wonderful leadership skills. As I recall,
her team would do *anything* for her. I'd love to have her on
board. I've made several other changes within my direct
report leadership team, and I know she'd fit right in."

After their call, Emily promised to call her. Within the
hour, she called back to confirm that Caroline would love to
join the team in North Carolina. Caroline's only reservation
was her concern about the long-term
viability of the property. Just as Rob,
too, had expressed concerns about
having a place to land if things didn't
work out, she didn't want to be left
hanging with no exit plan. Emily
assured her that as long as Caroline
remained mobile and didn't care what
she did next or where, things would
work out. Because Emily had established quite a reputation as
a leader who both took care of her people and kept her prom-
ises, that assurance was all Caroline needed. She was all in.

> *Execution of the
> fundamentals, the
> basics, no matter
> what the business,
> is a non-negotiable.*

His "people" plan was now in place, his vision had been
fully communicated and embraced, the hotel had been
drained of its Energy Vampires, and the customer council
had provided invaluable best practice and constructive feedback insights. Rob now firmly believed it was just a matter
of time before The Harper Hotel's North Carolina property
reestablished itself as a premier destination.

17. Leave a Legacy

Over the next several months, Rob consistently shared The Harper's vision with every new hire. He brought Bill Sebastian on board to consult whenever he lined up new-hire interviews. He wanted to ensure they were hiring for attitude, not just aptitude. The team could then collectively focus on the daily execution of its mission, which they eventually adopted during an off-site meeting. "*BYB*," short for "Bring Your Best," as in *every day, to everything you do.* Your best attitude, the best of your talent, your best service, and your very best effort. A commitment in each and every moment to deliver memorable experiences. Rob loved the mission statement because it was short yet powerful. It was shared with every new hire, and the expectation was clear. The Harper wanted staff committed to bringing their best in pursuit of excellence each and every day, and if you couldn't commit to bringing your best, stay home. With that attitude and commitment, together, they would make it happen.

On the personal front, regular visits from his wife and daughters for long weekends and several trips back to Chicago had helped keep Rob energized and focused. He and his wife had both begun calling the mountain community "home" for the past few weeks, and it was obvious after several visits that the rest of his family was falling in love with the area, too. The possibility of leaving Chicago no longer seemed so daunting.

Rob knew, as well, that his team needed a higher purpose longer term than simply self-preservation. They needed a connection to the community, one that extended beyond their business. Inspired by Newman's Own unorthodox philanthropy story in, *Shameless Exploitation in Pursuit of the Common Good*,[8] by Paul Newman, Rob began working with the local homeless shelter to form a partnership around the vision of eradicating homelessness in the community. The Harper would commit ten percent of its receipts to the shelter's work. Employees immediately loved and embraced the idea and many responded that it gave them a renewed sense of purpose, a reason to get out of bed in the morning and come to work.

One of the other concepts Rob introduced to the team was a bi-monthly "Lunch & Learn" initiative. Recognizing that folks came in over multiple shifts, he brought in Gary Blake— the bookstore owner who continued to be an inspiration and mentor to Rob—for one day every other month to facilitate a one-hour Lunch & Learn. They would review and discuss a book that Gary had selected and Rob had purchased for staff members. The sessions were voluntary, but as Rob reminded everyone, he expected people to take personal responsibility for becoming better versions of themselves. He knew that the only way The Harper would achieve a standard of excellence and become the very best possible version of itself was if the folks who worked there were committed to ongoing personal growth and improvement. The first book Gary selected was Mark Sanborn's *The Fred Factor*[9] a short but powerful story about going above and beyond the boundaries of your job description. There was no question that people knew what was expected. And they also knew that going above and beyond was rewarded. Rob and his direct reports were diligent when it came to catching people doing things *right*. Accomplishments were celebrated. He realized that waiting to celebrate until their vision had became a reality was too late. Just as fans cheer every great play and score along the way in any athletic contest, so, too, would he ensure that positive results were both recognized and rewarded along the way.

Rob's leadership team fostered an environment of empowerment. One of the many things Emily had taught him over the years was that you can't empower people, but you can create an environment where people feel empowered and then act accordingly. It was widely acknowledged that anyone on Team Harper had the authority to take care of any guest need, on the spot, no questions asked, and in fact the preference was that team members went out of their way to *anticipate* guest needs. Anticipating and creating memorable guest experiences became standard practice. Daily implementation of customer council feedback and best practice concepts took shape, and on top of that, Rob invited travel industry bloggers and writers onsite for a "Seeing is Believing" weekend. "The Harper experience," they wrote, "was unforgettable." The tide had turned.

Rob had even more to hope for and celebrate. His wife and daughters had spent the last weekend with him, relaxing and enjoying the area and dining with new friends, including Gary and Bill at Sebastian's. They talked honestly and openly about their wholehearted desire to make this town their new home if The Harper's turnaround success culminated in the board's decision to keep the property. With the six-month deadline fast approaching, Rob, his leadership team, and now his family and new friends, awaited the most current month-end metrics report, knowing full well that the board still reserved the right to pull the plug.

The grounds of The Harper had never been more beautiful. Finally, after six months of intentional and inspired teamwork, the insides had beauty to match. The "Dungeon" received a complete makeover, and had become a place where staff wanted to hang out on breaks. Rob had music piped in, new furniture delivered, and the walls were repainted a lighter, more vibrant color. And, the final change—symbolic of the culture changes that had come to pass during Rob's tenure: the old, dark, dank carpeting had been ripped up and hauled away. Everything was fresh, bright, and light.

Rob's philosophy of putting his employees first—and the customer second—was paying off. Happy employees = happy guests. Employee turnover had come to a grinding halt. Applications for open positions overwhelmed Rob's HR manager. Word of mouth within the hospitality industry in their corner of the world was that there was something very compelling and cool going on at The Harper, and people wanted to be part of it. Great leaders attract great talent, and Rob had hired some of the best folks out there to lead key teams throughout the hotel. Things couldn't be going any better.

Rob was always glad to see Cat—she was one of those folks who energized and uplifted him. But this Friday afternoon, as she entered his office, something just didn't seem right. She looked as if she had been crying. She asked if he had a few moments to talk. Rob closed his door and offered her a seat. He wasn't prepared for what came next.

Cat sat on the edge of the chair Rob offered, took a deep breath, and began. "First of all, I need to let you know that these last several months have been wonderful. You've made a tremendous impact on this place, our team, and for me personally. It's been an honor and a pleasure working with and for you. I know that under your leadership, this hotel will continue to flourish."

"Thank you, Cat," Rob responded. "I really do appreciate the words of affirmation. But I feel as if there's a "but" coming and, truthfully, I'm not sure I am ready for it."

"You're right, and I'm sorry, Rob. I'm here to tender my resignation. My husband has just been promoted and that means an immediate move to California. He begins next week. He loves his job and our kids are all grown, so we are mobile. And, as you know, his job pays the vast majority of our bills. I have always worked out of a love for

> *happy employees = happy guests*

what I do, never for the money. I know I will eventually find meaningful work on the West coast, but I've been spoiled here and it'll be hard to top the experiences and opportunities you have afforded me," Cat said. She'd been holding it together but now needed a tissue before continuing. "I'm sure you've read the great business book, *Who Moved My Cheese,* by Spencer Johnson, and that you'll get this metaphor: somebody 'moved my cheese.'[10] So, I'm going to choose to remain positive that I'm having to pursue "new cheese" in California. As important as this job is to me, my relationship with my husband and our life together must come first. I know you get that. I briefly considered allowing him to go on ahead of me, and following him later, but I feel strongly that I need to be there for him from the beginning. I do hope you understand."

"Of course, Cat," Rob replied. "I truly do understand. While I am happy for you and your husband, there is a selfish side of me that realizes your leaving will create a huge void here. We can replace your position, but we will never find another Catherine. You have made a lasting impact on the lives of so many people—not just our guests, but our staff, as well. I know that you know this, but there isn't a day that goes by without someone coming up to me to share a story about you. Your influence, your imprint, who you are being when you are doing what you are doing—it will all carry on. The work that you have done with the indoctrination of our new hires has been invaluable. You are leaving a lasting mark on this place, a legacy. And in the end, I'm not sure there is anything more important that we can accomplish in this life." Rob paused, too emotional to speak, then said, "I will never be able to thank you enough, but I can promise to protect, nurture, and share all that you have so passionately and generously offered. You are truly a rare jewel."

Cat and Rob embraced, and Cat left before any more tears were shed. Even though she knew that she was making the best decision for her family, she still felt like she was abandoning Rob. And as much as Rob was saddened and disappointed to be losing Cat, his first concern was for her, knowing how difficult it can be to leave a great workplace. He deeply empathized with her because only six months ago, he'd been in the same position. And someday, he would move on and his time at The Harper would be measured, not by his job title, how much money he made, or what car he drove, but by who he had been for others. He knew that as with Cat, legacies live on long after we're gone.

18. Everyone on Board

With the date of the board meeting only a few days away, Rob and his team pulled together the latest financials and other quantitative metrics that would prove that their six-month turnaround efforts had been worthwhile. That The Harper's North Carolina location should remain open under his leadership. Even as solid as the numbers were, the board could still decide to sell the property. As he had done with every other initiative since his arrival, Rob carefully and intentionally prepared for his time with the board, knowing he'd only get one small window of the hour-long meeting. And he was feeling the pressure. Anybody could present positive numbers, but their story went far beyond the numbers. The financial metrics were the end results of collective "hard" and "soft" efforts. He had concrete data to support his position, but he knew that people remembered stories long after they'd forgotten the numbers. He had a story he needed to tell, and he could only hope and pray that the board would move forward on a combination of faith and the foundation that he had helped to build.

   Emily called Rob to tell him the board meeting would be in North Carolina and that his property would host all twelve members for an evening dinner, an overnight stay, and the meeting that following morning. Rob had two days to make his final mental and physical preparations. He called an all-staff meeting and shared the great news, that they would get their chance to shine and show the board that both this team and this property were world class. He reminded them of how far they had all come together, and that they—using a football analogy—were inside the five-yard line with time winding down and a last shot at puting the ball across the goal line.

⚜

The evening of the board's arrival coincided, fortuitously, with The Harper's first sell-out in over two years. Occupancy rates had doubled in the last two months, but they had never reached one hundred percent occupancy. Timing was every-thing. The place was buzzing, the team was prepared, and Robbin had worked her magic behind the scenes to ensure that every guest experience would be memorable in some personal way. Dinner was exceptional, and after the board members retired for the evening, Rob called his leadership team together for one last huddle.

   "Tomorrow, the board will render a decision," Rob began. "It is now out of our hands. We have done everything we were called to do. And regardless of their decision, I want you to know this: I could not be more proud of our team. I had a vision six months ago that has, tonight, become a reality. And each of you has been incredibly instrumental in bringing our shared vision to fruition. It was no small feat. We have come a very long way together. And we have done it all the right way, living our values and proving that you can be successful in this business by treating people with dignity, respect, and love. I want to thank you for your investment of time, effort, and energy, but mostly, your heart. None of this would have been possible without heart."

With that, they all moved together into a tight circle of support and friendship. Tomorrow was a big day for each of them, and they knew—regardless of the board's final decision—they had accomplished something extraordinary.

19. The Decision

*B*y the time Rob had his ten minutes to address the board, he knew they'd already have reviewed the numbers. He was taking a huge risk with how he'd decided to spend his time, but had slept on his decision overnight and woke with the same belief that he'd be making the very best use of that time.

Today's board meeting would also be Cat's last day.

When the door to the meeting room opened and the board invited him in, Rob greeted everyone and gave a personal nod of assurance to Emily, who had been in attendance for the entire hour discussion on this property. Everyone expected that Rob would take his ten minutes to speak to the board about the last six months, and to provide justification and rationalization for why he should be given the opportunity to continue the good work he had started.

When Catherine walked into the room and Rob introduced her, the board members wondered to themselves why someone other than Rob—especially someone who wasn't part of the leadership team—would address them. Nobody said a word, but Rob could read body language. For a moment, he second-guessed his decision. But then Cat began to speak.

She spoke from her heart. She spoke about what she had learned and who she had become during the last six months, and the transformative changes she had witnessed. She talked about the investments made, not just in the physical environment and the building, but in the lives of those who called this place their work home. She shared that those now working at The Harper felt like family, and she spoke with glowing praise of the culture Rob had carefully and intentionally crafted. She shared that as difficult as it was going to be to walk out the doors one last time this morning, she felt good about her decision to move with her husband, and incredibly proud of what she was leaving behind. She said that, like herself, each and every member of the staff had given their very best to The Harper and they deserved more time to further prove that Rob's vision was both viable and sustainable, for the property, and for the entire company. Quite simply, she believed in Rob and his vision, and shared that there was an entire organization of folks who believed, as well.

"Ladies and gentlemen, now it's time for you to believe. Sometimes in life you must move forward on faith. And sometimes, you are fortunate enough to get outward and visible signs of positive change, both faith and proof. This is one of those times." And with that, Cat thanked the board for their time and left the room. Rob followed Cat out, closing the door behind them. He knew how much Cat disliked public speaking and how difficult those ten minutes had been for her. It must have felt like ten hours. Her time with the board members was her one last, final gift to him, to the team, and to The Harper. She had more than delivered.

"Thank you, Cat, from the bottom of my heart. I'm not sure how I can ever repay you," Rob said, as they slowly walked down the hall.

"You are so welcome, Rob. And please don't ever think about it in terms of repayment. There isn't anything that I wouldn't do for you, or for our team. These last six months have been your gift to me. Thanks for believing in me, and for allowing me the opportunity to share my gifts with others. Let me know what the board decides, but know this. Either way, we have done what we set out to do, and I'll always be proud of what we have accomplished together. Thank you, for everything."

Rob hugged Cat one last time. And as she walked away, he knew she wouldn't look back, and he knew he would never forget her.

⚜

Rob returned to his office to await the board's decision. Just before they adjourned at noon, he was invited back in. He looked first at Emily, thinking she'd give away the decision with some subtle expression, but she maintained a look of studied indifference and he couldn't read anything from her face. He had no idea what was to happen next.

The board president began to speak. "Rob, we believe in you. We believe in your team. We believe in this property. And know this—it's not as much about all of the great numbers we've had an opportunity to review, or what we have come to understand about what you and your team have been able to accomplish here—as it is about *how* you did it. Many people can manage, few can lead. Thank you for modeling a fresh and inspired new way forward, not just for this location, but for our entire company. Please do us the honor of letting everyone here know how much we appreciate each individual effort that collectively made this day—and this decision—possible. We look forward to watching you and your team continue to do great work. Congratulations!"

Rob thanked the board and shook hands with each member. He then walked over to Emily, hugged her, and thanked her for maintaining a straight face so that he would forever remember the moment the board president gave him the gift of an exciting future with The Harper in the mountains. On a more serious note, he thanked her for her investment of time and her belief in him and his team. He was reminded in the moment, once again, that nobody ever achieves anything worthwhile alone. He then excused himself from the meeting room.

He had a team he wanted to share the wonderful news with, and a family to move to the mountains.

Afterword

*I*n my travels, I thoroughly enjoy encounters with people who make my day, folks who are remarkable not for what they do, but for how they do it. I wish these "WOW" experiences were not so rare, which makes the principles in this book even more critical to share. Most people know, but few apply, the lessons that Rob comes to learn in *No Reservations*.

I find that many in the service industry are focused on the transaction, not on the relationship. My hope is that the messages in this book positively influence the lives of those who take the time to read and live out the lessons in a way that can have a transformative ripple effect.

I'd love to hear your stories and examples of people you meet who go above and beyond their position descriptions to make a difference in this world. I look forward to highlighting them on my website and Facebook page.

Blessings!

Todd Gothberg
website: ToddGothberg.com
Facebook: facebook.com/toddgothbergpage
Twitter: Gberg8

1. Choose to be positive
2. Make their day
3. Invest in you
4. Pursue excellence
5. Be remarkable
6. Be present
7. Be intentional
8. Be kind and thoughtful
9. Live your values
10. Leave a legacy

Pictured: Dr. Lisa Greene, Sister Lucia, and the author outside Casa Moraga

Ten percent of the proceeds from the sale of this book will go to support the work of Almas Unidas—Hearts United, and Casa Moraga, an orphanage for girls in El Salvador.

almasunidas-heartsunited.org

Endnotes

1. "Faith and Fear have something in common, they both believe in a future that hasn't yet happened." Jon Gordon, jongordon.com.

2. *It's Not About the Coffee—Leadership Principles From a Life at Starbucks.* Howard Behar with Janet Goldstein. Penguin Group (USA), 2007.

3. "Get to vs. Have to." *The No Complaining Rule: Positive Ways to Deal with Negativity at Work.* Jon Gordon. Wiley; first edition, 2008.

4. "Be Kind and Thoughtful." Inspired by the philosophy of Newman's Own: newmansownfoundation.org.

5. *Live Your Values: Wooden: A Lifetime of Observations and reflections On and Off the Court.* Coach John Wooden with Steve Jamison. Contemporary Books; first edition, 1997.

6. *The New Gold Standard—5 Leadership Principles for Creating a Legendary Customer Experience Courtesy of The Ritz-Carlton Hotel Company.* Joseph A. Michelli. McGraw-Hill; first edition, 2008.

7. *Good to Great: Why Some Companies Make the Leap ... and Others Don't.* Jim Collins. HarperBusiness; first edition, 2001.

8. *Shameless Exploitation in Pursuit of the Common Good: The Madcap Business Adventure by the Truly Oddest Couple.* Paul Newman and A.E. Hotchner. Nan A. Talese; first edition, 2003.

9. *The Fred Factor: How passion in your work and life can turn the ordinary into the extraordinary.* Mark Sanborn. Currency; first edition, 2004.

10. *Who Moved My Cheese?: An A-Mazing Way to Deal with Change in Your Work and in Your Life.* Spencer Johnson. G. P. Putnam's Sons; first edition, 1998.

Index

About the Author

Todd Gothberg

*Author • Speaker • Culture Change
Coach • Facilitator*

*T*odd is a sought after keynote speaker, trainer, CEO Coach, and process facilitator who brings expertise on a number of topics, including Exceptional Leadership, Employee Engagement, Effective Communication, Positive Cultures, Team Dynamics, Health & Wellness, Time Management, and Customer Loyalty. Todd has thirty years of practical business experience in a variety of capacities and disciplines. Todd holds a BA in Business Management from Gettysburg College in Gettysburg, Pennsylvania, and an MBA with a concentration in Organizational Behavior from Lebanon Valley College in Annville, Pennsylvania.

On the personal side, Todd is raising three beautiful daughters (born: 1991, 1994, and 2000), and he recently competed for Team USA at the World Triathlon Championships in Australia. He is a four-time Ironman finisher, and has completed more than forty marathons since 1989.

Often requested speaking topics:
- Employee Engagement/Team Dynamics
- Effective Communication
- Building Positive Cultures
- Time Management
- No Reservations: Building Customer Loyalty, One Relationship at a Time

Culture Change Coach
- Onsite culture assessments and training
- Leading through change

Xerox Certified Process Facilitator
- One-on-one and small-group focus facilitation
- Leadership and executive facilitation

Todd is a leader of leaders who inspires others to reach toward their full potential and to make improvements, both personally and professionally. He can move from the board room to the trenches and have an impact in both areas. He lives his life's purpose and has a strong value set, which is his guiding compass.
—Michael Womble II, Regional
Fleet Sales at Volvo Trucks

Todd is highly skilled at developing and building dynamic teams by encouraging and inspiring a true passion for excellence. Because of work with him, our values influenced our strategy, formed the basis of our practices, guided the behavior of our team, and provided a sense of vision and inspiration.
—Anna Christine Sgro, Vice President,
Ritchie Bros. Auctioneers, Canada

To request more information, or to contact Todd:
email: toddgothberg@gmail.com
website: toddgothberg.com
facebook: facebook.com/toddgothbergpage

Courtesy of Jon Gordon

Jon Gordon - Best Selling Author & Keynote Speaker

Jon Gordon's best-selling books and talks have inspired readers and audiences around the world. His principles have been put to the test by numerous NFL, NBA, and college coaches and teams, Fortune 500 companies, school districts, hospitals, and non-profits. He is the author of *The Wall Street Journal* bestseller *The Energy Bus, The No Complaining Rule, Training Camp, The Shark and the Gold-fish, Soup, The Seed* and his latest *The Positive Dog*. Jon and his tips have been featured on The Today Show, CNN, Fox and Friends and in numerous magazines and newspapers. His clients include The Atlanta Falcons, Campbell Soup, Wells Fargo, State Farm, Novartis, Bayer and more.

Jon is a graduate of Cornell University and holds a Masters in Teaching from Emory University. He and his training/consulting company are passionate about developing positive leaders, organizations and teams.

When he's not running through airports or speaking to businesses, hospitals or school leaders, you can find him playing tennis or lacrosse with his wife and two teenage children.

Todd Gothberg

At Volvo Construction Equipment, Todd serves as Director of Employee Engagement and Customer Satisfaction leading North American employee and dealer efforts ensuring Volvo secures a #1 position in Customer Satisfaction. He also supports the personal and leadership development training for the Volvo and its dealerships within the Dealer Development team.

Todd is a sought after key note speaker on a variety of topics, including Leadership, Effective Communication, Building Positive Cultures, Team Dynamics, Health & Wellness, Time Management/ Prioritization, and Customer Loyalty. Todd authored *No Reservations*, a business fable about building customer loyalty one relationship at a time, which published last November.

Todd holds a BA in Business Management from Gettysburg College in Gettysburg, PA and an MBA with a concentration in Organizational Behavior, from Lebanon Valley College.

On the personal side, Todd is raising three beautiful daughters (23, 20, 13), competed for Team USA at the World Triathlon Championships in Australia, has completed 41 marathons, the Spartan Ultra-Beast and 4 Ironman competitions.

SHIPPENSBURG AREA CHAMBER OF COMMERCE & VOLVO CE PRESENT:

LEADERSHIP CONFERENCE

Wednesday, January 22, 2014
6:00pm-9:00pm

6:00pm — **Scott Brown**, *Shippensburg Area Chamber of Commerce-Executive Director*

Todd Gothberg, *Volvo CE-Director of Employee Engagement & Customer Satisfaction*

6:05pm — **Dinner**

6:45pm — **A Word from Our Sponsor: Chuck Wood**, *Volvo CE-Vice President of Human Resource Management & Administration*

7:00pm — **Speaker: Todd Gothberg, author of "No Reservations"**

7:20pm — **Carol Cantele**, *Gettysburg College-Head Women's Lacrosse Coach/Assistant Athletic Director*

7:25pm — **Speaker: Jon Gordon, author of "The Energy Bus"**

8:30pm — **Book Signing**

Thank you to Volvo CE for co-sponsoring & Shippensburg University for hosting this event!